C000044159

THE MASTER GARDENER'S GUIDE TO

CREATIVE
GARDEN
PROJECTS

RICHARD WILES

SELECT
EDITIONS

A SALAMANDER BOOK

©1986 Salamander Books Ltd.

This edition published 1991 by
Selectabook Ltd.,
Folly Road,
Roundway,
Devizes,
Wiltshire, U.K.
SN10 2HR.

ISBN 0 86101 245 3

Credits
Editor: Jonathan Elphick
Designs: Richard Wiles
Art Editor: Tony Domini
Filmset: Modern Text Ltd

Colour reproductions:
Rodney Howe Ltd.
Printed in Belgium by
Henri Proost & Cie, Turnhout

AUTHOR

Richard Wiles has been a professional writer and designer for over ten years, and is the author of numerous books and articles on practical projects for the garden and the home. He has contributed to most of the leading British periodicals in this field, accumulating considerable experience of design considerations and construction techniques, and of describing them for the general reader.

CONTENTS

Nature's not always orderly or tidy, and it's up to you, the gardener, to tame its wilder tendencies. A plot resplendent with colourful blooms, a lush green lawn and well-defined flower beds doesn't just come about naturally; it's necessary to style it as you'd like it—whether it's a practical patch for vegetables, a display case for flowers or simply somewhere to recline in summer.

PLOT WITH A PURPOSE

Whether you've just taken over a garden with a new house, you're starting from scratch with an unkempt area left by the builders, or you just want to ring the changes with your old plot, your priority is to decide what purpose the garden is to fulfil.

List what you want from your garden, taking into account your outdoor activities, interests and family needs. Include the permanent features—patio, path, shrubbery, shed—plus the short-term items: a sandpit for the children for instance.

Choose a style for the plot: if

you're keen on cultivation, opt for a semi-formal set-up of flower beds, lawn, rockery and green-house (or a more flamboyant, wild style of undergrowth lush with shrubs and trees); if you're practically-minded, give over a substantial chunk of the garden to vegetable-growing; if you're blatantly lazy, you could plan for nothing more than a leisure area, with a patio, barbecue and shady bower.

Once you've chosen the theme for your garden, consider whether the existing site fits the bill, or whether drastic redevelopment is necessary. There are many ways to adapt the site to suit your ends, for example by defining new areas with walls or fences (see pages 18-33), substituting areas of lawn for paved surfaces (see pages 38-43) or containing flower beds and shrubbery in timber or brick planters (see pages 54-55).

Although you're stuck with the overall size and shape of the garden, if the profile of the ground doesn't comply with your design, it's possible to remodel even this to make a gently

rolling, terraced or split-level arrangement—or just flatten a steeply-sloping site.

While you plan the garden, pay heed to the health and welfare of the soil: don't excavate the ground to the detriment of decent drainage, which is essential for the livelihood of all that grows in it (see page 12).

YOUR PLANS AND THE LAW

The following brief account of the legal aspects of planning applies to the current situation in the United Kingdom. In other countries, planning laws differ, and you should make sure that your proposed work complies with your local planning and building regulations.

Planning rules cover the way land is developed, particularly the construction of extensions, and other visible work outside, too. Much of the work you're likely to do is classified as 'permitted development' and no approval is needed if the work complies with size and location restrictions.

Fences and walls need planning permission if they are

Above: *This well-designed garden features an attractive patio area.*

more than 3ft 3in (1m) high along a boundary or highway used by vehicular traffic, or 6ft 6in (2m) elsewhere in the garden. Hedges are exempt from planning control.

Hardstanding for a car does not need approval so long as it is within your property and the vehicle is mainly for private use.

An outbuilding (including a shed or swimming pool) does not need approval as long as it is not used for business; if no part projects beyond the building line of a house facing a highway; if it is no more than 13ft (4m) high with a ridged roof, or 10ft (3m) high otherwise; and if not more than half the garden will be covered by building structures.

Tree felling or lopping is permitted unless the tree is protected by a Tree Preservation Order (TPO), or if you live in a conservation area.

Means of access—a path or a driveway—to the road requires permission (unless onto an unclassified road).

SHAPING THE GROUND

Changes in the level of a garden can be attractive, but are often a chore to work and frequently suffer from soil erosion and ultimately feeble plant growth. A flat plot may be beset with inadequate drainage. Whatever the lie of the land, remodelling the earth to improve poor conditions—or simply to open up a fresh aspect—is quite straightforward, if laborious.

PLANNING THE SHAPE

Altering the shape of your garden basically involves removing soil from high ground and using it to fill low ground. Nevertheless, you must be careful not to disrupt the natural structure of the earth or problems of drainage, and even stability, could ensue.

Don't attempt a massive excavation, working instead within practical boundaries: if a steep bank makes access prohibitive with lawnmower and wheelbarrow, for instance, or if it drains towards the house, try to lessen the angle or form a series of terraces.

If you're creating a new bank, make sure the angle is no steeper than about 30°, or the topsoil will be eroded by rain, and underground water movement could cause sinking.

Improve a totally flat site by carving gentle hollows and subtle rises, or create a split-level effect with shallow steps flanked by low retaining walls.

CUTTING AND FILLING

To reshape the ground, dig out the topsoil at the high level to about 6in (150mm) and set it aside. Repeat for the low level. Dig out the subsoil from the high level to the depth required.

Transport the earth by wheelbarrow to the low level and tip it over the excavated area. Spread the soil with a rake, then compact it with a roller or stamp over it with the heels of your boots. Fill any indents, then replace the topsoil at the top and bottom of the bank.

LEVELLING BY PEGS AND PLANK

If you're going to cast a foundation slab—for a shed, for instance (see page 16), you'll need a fairly flat, level and well-drained area. On ground that's not too undulating, level the surface using timber datum pegs and

Below: *If you find a sloping site* **(A)** *difficult to work or simply boring, remodel it to create a terraced effect* **(B).**

Previous level

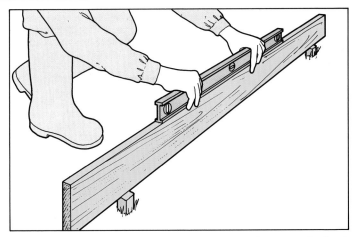

a long builder's spirit level.

Choosing the site that involves the least excavation, drive a 12in (300mm) long, 1in (25mm) square peg—the prime datum— into the ground using a club hammer, so that the top of the peg is at the level you want the entire plot to be. Sink more pegs into the ground over the area at 5ft (1·5m) intervals. Rest one end of a long plank on the first peg and the other end on the nearest peg. Place a spirit level on top of the plank and adjust the depth of the second peg until the spirit level registers horizontal. Repeat the process for the remaining pegs, working across the site.

When all pegs are set to the prime datum, excavate the soil until it is level with their tops. Tramp over the surface to high-light voids, fill them with more soil using the cut-and-fill method, then rake flat. If you've a shortage of soil, import some from a garden centre.

USING A WATER LEVEL

Rough ground will forbid the use of pegs and plank, so adopt the water level method: water finds its own level, so use your ordinary garden hose as a measuring device.

Insert a short length of clear

Above: *Drive in pegs to the level you want for the site, align them with a spirit level and plank, then dig out the ground to their tops.*

plastic tubing into each end of the hose and mark a line around it to serve as a gauge, using a felt-tipped pen. Fill the hose with water—from a watering can minus rose—and hold (or tape) one end against a datum peg.

Hold the other end of the hose against a peg at the other side of the site. Align the gauge marks with the peg tops and adjust the depth at which the pegs are sunk until the levels are the same at both ends. Dig out the bulk of the soil between the pegs, fix intermediate pegs and level the whole site.

Above: *Adjust peg depths until the water levels are the same.*

DRAINAGE

A poorly drained garden is not only detrimental to plant and shrub growth—specimens will be stunted, prone to rot at the roots and bouts of mildew—but also swelling and shrinkage of the subsoil can cause cracks in the house walls and, in severe cases, subsidence of the foundations. Installing artificial drainage may restore the balance.

DIGGING A DRAINAGE TRENCH

If your drainage problem is not severe, alleviate it by installing land drains. These can be simple gravel-filled trenches or a network of plastic, pitch-fibre, concrete or unglazed clay pipes feeding a soakaway (see below).

The trench must be set at the correct gradient if it is to drain efficiently: a gentle, consistent slope of 1:40 is best to prevent water washing along it.

Using string stretched between pegs to mark out the trenches. Remove the topsoil or slice out rectangles of turf and set aside. Dig a trench about a spade's width across and about 1ft 4in (400mm) deep at the top; the depth at the bottom of the run depends on the gradient. Use a long plank to check that the trench slopes consistently.

Put about 6in (150mm) of hardcore (broken bricks or concrete) or coarse gravel into the base as a water filter. Top this with about 2in (50mm) of coarse sand, then compact the surface by stamping with your boots. Return the topsoil or turfs.

CALCULATING THE GRADIENT

Use a water level (see page 11) to work out the gradient: drive pegs into the ground at the top and bottom of the slope with 1ft (300mm) protruding and mark off 6in (150mm) from the top of each; tape the hose between

them, then fill it with water. The water will reach the line on the lowest end first; continue to add water until it reaches the second line. Measure the distance above the first line and the distance between the two pegs to find the gradient. For example: where the height difference is 2in (50mm) and the pegs are 16ft (5m) apart, the gradient is 1:50.

LAYING LAND DRAINS

If you are laying drain pipes, prepare the trench in the same way, but set them out in a herringbone pattern. The spine should lead to a soakaway, with branches fanning from it.

Drain pipes measure either 3in

Top: *Dig the trenches, then lay drain pipes end to end and cover the joints with polythene.*
Above: *Sprinkle gravel over the pipes, then replace topsoil.*

or 4in (75mm or 100mm) in diameter; use the large size for the spine, the smaller one for the branches. Choose either perforated or unperforated pipes: the former allow surplus water to filter away. Plastic pipes are sold in considerable lengths and can be bent to avoid obstacles (boulders and tree roots); clay 'field' pipes are cheap, in 1ft 4in (400mm) lengths, but require an angle grinder to cut them.

Lay the pipes in the trenches, end-to-end (perforated types holes down; unperforated ones with ⅜in (10mm) gaps between them, so water can seep in). Cover each joint with a square of tough polythene, so earth will not silt up the pipes. Top with gravel cover with 6in (150mm) of topsoil, and replace any turfs.

MAKING A SOAKAWAY

A soakaway is basically a pit filled with rubble, which filters water back to the earth. Position it at the bottom of the gradient, and extend the spine of the pipework into it for about 1ft (300mm).

Dig out the topsoil and any

Below: *Calculate the gradient using a water level; the height difference in relation to the slope length gives the ratio.*

turfs and set aside. Excavate a hole about 4ft (1·2m) square and about 3ft (1m) deeper than the incoming pipe. Provided this extends to below the first layer of subsoil, it will reach the better-draining lower layers; otherwise your soakaway will fill up with water. You may need to dig as much as 6ft (2m).

Tip hardcore and rubble into the pit to the level of the pipe then use a sledgehammer to compact it. Cover the rubble with a layer of coarse gravel, then add a sheet of loft insulation so the topsoil won't wash down and clog the filter. Roll the surface and return the topsoil, then returf or plant out the area.

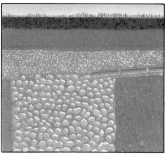

Above: *The soakaway is a pit 3ft (1m) deeper than the incoming pipe, filled with rubble, topped with gravel to filter water away.*

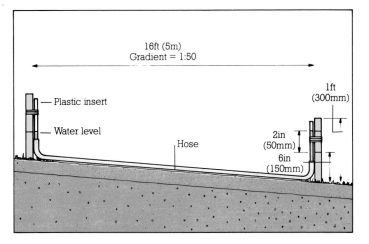

16ft (5m)
Gradient = 1:50

1ft (300mm)

Plastic insert

Water level

Hose

2in (50mm)

6in (150mm)

FOUNDATIONS

Any structure you build in the garden needs adequate foundations to support it and spread its load to firm ground. Whether you're building a garden wall to define different areas or casting a concrete drive, the principles are similar.

MAKING STRIP FOUNDATIONS

Foundations for a garden wall are set in a trench filled with a layer of compacted hardcore topped with concrete. The depth of the strip depends on the height and thickness of the wall, and on the soil condition. Basically, the weaker the subsoil, the deeper the trench.

The foundation is built wider than the wall, because the weight of the wall is spread out at an angle of 45°. So, make the width of the foundation at each side of the wall at least equal to the depth of the concrete.

For a wall over about six courses high, dig a trench about 20in (500mm) deep, whereas for a smaller wall twice the depth of concrete will do, unless the soil is soft.

SETTING OUT THE FOUNDATIONS

Set up profile boards at each end of the site. Hammer pairs of pegs 24in (600mm) long x 2in sq (50mm sq) into the ground at each end of the wall line. Nail

24in (600mm) long cross-pieces of 2in x 1in (50mm x 25mm) timber on top.

Attach nails to each cross-piece the width of the trench apart. Tie a stringline between the nails. Sprinkle sand over the strings to leave a trail on the ground to show where to dig. Remove the strings but leave the boards as a guide to laying the bricks (see pages 18-21).

Dig the trench to the depth required (check this every 3ft/1m), then drive timber pegs at 24in (600mm) intervals along the centre of the trench so they protrude by the depth of concrete. Span the pegs with a spirit level to ensure they're horizontal.

Tip hardcore into the trench and ram it to the same thickness as the concrete. Mix a load of concrete comprising 1 part cement; 2½ parts sand; 3½ parts aggregate (or 5 parts all-in aggregate) and shovel it on top of the hardcore.

Use a stout length of timber to tamp the mix level with the peg tops, dispelling air bubbles that would weaken the concrete. Check the level of the strip with a spirit level, make any adjustments, then cover the foundation with polythene sheeting and leave to harden for 24 hours before building on it.

Below: *Mark out strip foundations with profile boards comprising pairs of pegs with cross-pieces; strings denote the trench sides.*

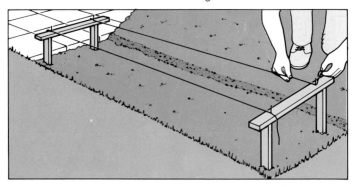

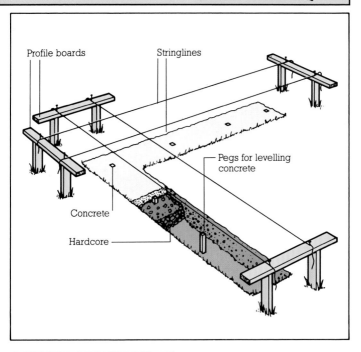

USING CONCRETE

Concrete is a durable, tough material which can be used in making foundations, either as a sub-base for another building material, or as a surface in its own right. It's made by mixing Portland cement with the aggregates sand, gravel or stones, and water. The water and cement form a paste which binds the bulk-making aggregate together.

Cement comes in 1cwt (50kg) bags; sand, gravel and stones are sold loose, separately or mixed as all-in aggregate.

For strip foundations, mix the concrete by hand, but you will find this method too laborious for raft foundations (see page 16).

Tip the cement over the aggregate, form a crater, then add half the water by bucket. Collapse the sides of the heap and mix it by turning it over several times. Test the consistency of the mix by running your shovel across it in steps: the ridges should be firm and slump-free.

Above: *Set up profile boards, dig the trench then drive pegs into the base protruding by the concrete thickness. Add the compact hardcore then concrete levelled to the peg tops.*

Below: *Mix the water thoroughly with the sand, cement and aggregate to achieve an even slump-free concrete consistency.*

FOUNDATIONS

Strip foundations are fine for single walls, but bulkier structures—a coal bunker or garden building, for instance—and large, flat areas, such as a patio, path or drive, need more substantial support. Often the top of the foundation doubles as a finished surface in its own right.

FOUNDATIONS FOR PAVING

Any paving material—concrete slabs, block pavers or cast concrete—needs to be laid on a firm, flat base that will not subside. At its most basic, the foundation for a path or area of slabs can be well-compacted subsoil, but where the ground is soft, add a layer of hardcore first and consolidate this with a roller.

Even when compacted, hardcore will contain some voids, so fill these by covering the entire surface with a blinding layer of sand or lean concrete mix (1 part cement; 3 parts sand). Spread it flat with the back of a rake.

Slabs can be laid directly on the blinding layer on five dabs, or a complete bed, or mortar. Some types of paving block or brick can be laid directly on a bed of sand, spread over firm ground or hardcore (see pages 38-43).

Below: *Raft foundations comprise hardcore, sand to fill voids and concrete moulded and levelled in formwork fixed to stakes.*

FOUNDATIONS FOR GARDEN STRUCTURES

A lightweight garden shed or solid fuel bunker can simply be laid on a foundation comprising slabs over firmly-compacted earth or hardcore, but larger structures —a garage, for instance—require a solid surface of cast concrete. The concrete itself can be laid directly on firm earth, but fill any hollows with hardcore.

First clear the site of weeds, roots and large stones. Dig out the topsoil and set aside for re-use elsewhere in the garden. How far down you dig depends on where you want the finished surface of the foundation to be, taking into account adjoining features—the house damp-proof course (DPC), an existing path or lawn, for example.

Mark out the overall shape of the foundation with strings stretched between wooden pegs. Concrete must be laid within supporting formwork, to mould and retain the wet mix until it sets hard; make this frame from lengths of straight-edged planks about ½in (12mm) thick.

Nail the planks to stakes driven into the ground outside the area of the foundation. The formwork should be the depth required for the concrete, although you can wedge it up on bricks if necessary, so that the top is at the correct level.

Use a spirit level on a long

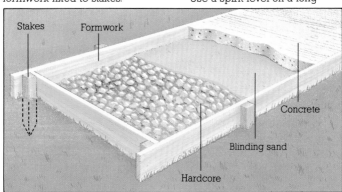

Stakes Formwork

Concrete

Blinding sand

Hardcore

straight edged plank to check that the boards are set at the same level: on large areas, incorporate a crossfall for drainage by placing a small offcut of wood—a shim—under the lower end of the level.

You'll also need a builder's square to set the stringlines and formwork perfectly square.

MAKING A BUILDER'S SQUARE

A builder's square is invaluable for checking that the corners of your foundation formwork are at true right-angles. Cut three pieces of 2in x 1in (50mm x 25mm) softwood into 12in, 16in and 20in (300mm, 400mm and 500mm) lengths and join the ends of the shortest together with a half-lap joint. Screw the long brace diagonally on top; the corner between the short pieces must be precisely at 90°.

MIXING BY MACHINE

Slab-type raft foundations will probably be too large for you to consider mixing concrete by hand, so hire a petrol- or electric-driven mixing machine.

To mix by machine, add half the aggregate by bucket to the revolving drum, followed by half the water by hose fitted with an isolating nozzle. Tip in the remaining ingredients and operate the mixer until the concrete falls cleanly off the blades.

CASTING THE CONCRETE MIX

Tip the concrete into the formwork and slice into it with your shovel to force it well down, dispelling any air pockets.

Using the back of a rake, level the mix roughly, just above the top of the formwork. Place a stout timber beam across the formwork and work it across the concrete with a chopping motion (you'll need assistance for this), followed by a sawing motion, to level and compact the mix.

If you are building on the slab, leave the rough finish caused by the tamping beam; if the concrete is to be on show, smooth it by running a steel trowel over the surface once the mix has begun to stiffen.

Cover the concrete with polythene and leave this in place for about three days until the surface is hard.

Above: *If you are mixing large amounts of concrete, hire a motorized mixer to take the toil out of the job. Set up the machine close to the foundations—you may be able to tip the mix directly into the formwork—otherwise, have a tough builder's barrow on hand.*

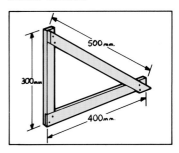

Above: *Make a builder's square from three lengths of softwood, and use it to check that the formwork is set at 90°.*

BRICK AND BLOCK WALLS

Walls and other types of enclosures are not just used to identify the boundaries of your property—they'll also protect against the elements, stifle traffic noise and screen an unattractive view. Used within the plot, they serve to define different areas —and will even hold back the earth in a split-level site. Bricks offer versatility in texture and colour and they're equally well suited to a formal or more relaxed setting, but if you'd prefer a more natural look, decorative walling blocks provide a more rugged appearance.

CHOOSING BRICKS AND BLOCKS

Bricks are moulded from fire-burnt clay in standard metric units 225 x 112·5 x 75mm. There are numerous brick types, but only three are suitable for walling: **Facing bricks** (stocks), for an attractive finish, are made in various colours with rough or smooth textures. 'Faced' versions have one or two attractive sides. **Common bricks,** where appearance isn't vital, are less costly. They have no special facing, are best when painted or rendered and shouldn't be subjected to heavy stress or loads. **Engineering bricks** are dense, smooth and impervious to water. Use them where a wall is likely to be exposed to damp conditions, or part of the wall buried below ground.

Decorative walling blocks are moulded from concrete, often with natural stone aggregates added for a more authentic appearance. They're split or pitched on one long and one short face, and made in greens, reds, greys, yellows and buff tones.

Various sizes are available and there are also modular blocks, moulded to resemble several smaller coursed stones, which can be used just like the single versions.

WORKING WITH BRICKS AND BLOCKS

With bricks and blocks, you can build a straight, curved or angular wall quite easily, from one a couple of courses high, that will

Below: *This Japanese-inspired garden, with areas of gravel, stones and paving slabs, blends with a brick wall supported by piers.*

18

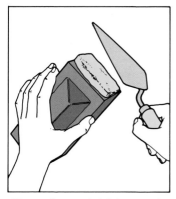

Above: *Butter a brick by scraping the mortar off the trowel; form a wedge-shape and furrow the top.*

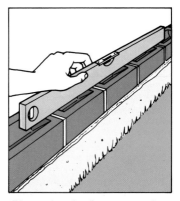

Above: *Lay the first course of bricks on mortar and use a spirit level to check for alignment.*

enhance the shape of a planting area, to a substantial barrier several feet in height.

Bricks are laid overlapping to provide a staggered bond for rigidity and to spread the wall's load to the foundations. The simplest is the stretcher bond (for single-thickness walls), where bricks are butted end-to-end and overlap by half on alternative courses; more complex bonds (for double-thickness walls) comprise courses of stretchers (bricks laid end-to-end) alternated with courses of headers (bricks laid across the width of the wall), which produce a decorative effect as well as reinforcing the structure. Part bricks maintain the regularity of a bond.

Blocks are laid similarly, except that for a double-thickness wall, it is necessary to build two leaves, as there is only one textured side.

Bricks and blocks are laid using a sand and cement mortar mix to glue them together. Buy dry pre-mixed bricklaying mortar for modest-sized jobs, but for substantial walls, it is more economical to mix your own using separate ingredients in the proportions 1 part cement : 6 parts builder's sand. A 1cwt (50kg) pre-mixed bag of mortar will lay about sixty bricks; the

Above: *Build up the lapping courses to a stringline running along the outside top edge.*

Above: *A long wall requires a supporting pier at intervals, bonded into the brickwork.*

same of cement, mixed in the above proportions, should cope with about 450 bricks.

DESIGN YOUR WALL

Decide what function the wall is to serve, then sketch out a plan of your plot, including the structure. Consider its length, route and height, taking into account permitted development (see page 9). Use strings and pegs to mark out the position of the wall on site so that you can visualize it.

The type of bond you choose depends on how decorative you'd like it to be, its rigidity, and economy—complicated bonds gobble up bricks and are wasteful in cut ones. Dry-lay the first four courses to test the bond.

If the wall is to be longer than about 6ft (1·8m) in half-brick stretcher bond, or 9ft (2·8m) in single brick bonding, build a supporting pier that projects by a least half a brick or block, using half-bricks and three-quarter bricks at alternate courses to maintain the bonding pattern.

CUTTING BRICKS AND BLOCKS

Bricks and blocks are easy to cut, using a club hammer and bolster chisel. Mark the amount to be cut off, then score the brick or block with the chisel. Place on a bed of sand (or on grass) and strike sharply on the scored line, chisel angled towards the waste to make a clean break. With split-faced blocks some irregularity is more authentic.

LAYING BRICKS AND BLOCKS

Bricks and blocks are laid in much the same way. Lay them on your concrete strip foundation (see page 14), using the profile boards as a guide to positioning. Tap nails into the cross pieces, centred, the width of the wall

Above: *Use a gauge rod made from a length of wood marked in brick-plus-joint increments to check that courses rise consistently*

Above: *Score a brick with a bolster chisel, place it on sand, then strike sharply to break.*

Above: *Check that the wall is not bowing by holding a spirit level diagonally against the face; tap top courses back into line.*

apart. Trowel a ⅝in (15mm) thick screed of mortar between the strings, then hold a spirit level vertically against each and transfer their positions to the screed as a scored line. Furrow the screed to aid adhesion.

Position the first brick or block at one end of the foundation and tap it down with the handle of your trowel. Scoop up the excess mortar that has been squeezed out and re-use it. Lay the second brick or block at the other end of the strip, or about six lengths away on a long wall, span the two with a long timber straight-edge and check their level with a spirit level; tap down the second one so the two are horizontal.

To fill in the intermediate units, butter the end of a third with mortar by scraping it off the trowel. Form a wedge shape and furrow the top, then butt the brick or block up to the end of the first laid one. Lay subsequent ones until you complete the first course. Check that the course is horizontal, adjust any bricks or blocks that aren't level, then hold the level alongside to test the alignment.

Build up the ends of the wall to six courses, forming a stepped arrangement. Check that the courses are consistently spaced using a gauge rod—a 3ft (1m) length of 2 x ½in (50 x 12mm) softwood marked off in brick or block-plus-joint increments. Fill in the intermediate units,

Above: *These simulated stone walls, incorporating graceful curves, combine well with a gravel area.*

checking frequently for alignment and squareness. Use a stringline stretched along the wall, tied to two pins stuck in the mortar joints as a guide to laying horizontally: the string should run along the top outer edge. Raise the string at every course. At each course, hold the spirit level diagonally across the face of the wall to check for bowing.

POINTING THE JOINTS

The mortar joints must be shaped neatly to deflect rainwater, once the mortar has stiffened. The best profile for an exposed wall is the weatherstruck type: press in a neat V-shape with the edge of your trowel on the horizontals and verticals. A simpler profile is formed by running a length of dowel or plastic hose along the joints.

CAPPING AND COPING

Special-shaped bricks are made to finish off the top of a wall and to prevent rainwater from lying. Typical shapes include half-rounded or bevel-edged types.

To complete a blockwork wall, you can buy flat or bevelled coping stones, which are wider than the wall. Capping stones, to top a pier, are also available.

In a split-level garden a retaining wall prevents the earth from spilling out of its banked shape. The wall must be able to withstand considerable pressures and provision for draining the soil must be included. You can build a retaining wall in bricks or blocks, but these small-scale units tend to bulge under pressure; cast concrete solves the problem but can look utilitarian, while timber calls for regular maintenance. A dry stone wall, however, gives a naturally rugged look.

BUYING STONES

You can build dry stone retaining walls to create terraces on a steeply sloping site or to surround a raised bed in a flat garden. The wall should not be taller than 4ft (1·2m) without guidance from the local authority.

Suitable stones can be obtained from quarries and stone merchants. There are various types,

and choice depends on durability and how impervious to water it is. In general choose the hardest stone, such as granite or basalt. You can buy stone with regular, flat edges or irregularly shaped.

Colour is important if the wall is to blend with the character of the plot: hues range from rustic blue to grey and honey-coloured. You'll need about one tonne per cubic metre of wall.

PREPARING THE FOUNDATIONS

A dry stone wall is wedge-shaped, tapering from a broad base to a narrow top so its load is spread evenly. A retaining version only requires a 'batter' (tilt) on the outer face—this is set using two 'batter frames', each made from

Below: *The wall comprises large flat base stones, topped with edge blocks filled with irregular pieces and tied with long, flat stones spanning both leaves.*

four lengths of 2in sq (50mm sq) sawn timber: a vertical post with a horizontal cross batten top and bottom to brace a diagonal fixed between them—a slope of about 2in in 12in (50mm in 300mm) is adequate. Drive the vertical and diagonal into the ground at each end of the wall, then stretch string between as a guide to laying the stones; raise as you work.

Excavate the bank to form a vertical terrace against which to build the wall. If you're building on a flat site, prepare to back-fill with a considerable amount of earth, which will settle.

LAYING THE STONES

A small wall doesn't require concrete foundations—build it in a rubble-filled trench about 24in (600mm) deep, which allows drainage to the subsoil. Make the trench twice as wide as the top of the wall.

Start by laying a few courses of large flat stones in the base of the trench, interlocked, then add smaller edging stones at each side. Fill the cavity between with small irregular stones. Build in this way, forming the batter by angling each stone downwards into the bank. At random intervals, lay large, wide stones across the wall to bind the leaves. Some of these should project beyond the back of the wall to be buried in the earth as anchors.

Fill any gaps with chippings and soil, where plants can be inserted to help prevent soil erosion. At the top of the wall, fit a row of large flat stones to tie the leaves together, then top with coping stones laid on edge and tilting in one direction.

BACK-FILLING WITH EARTH

As you build the wall, back-fill with subsoil and pack it down lightly to fill voids. At the top, add a layer of topsoil and turfs or plants.

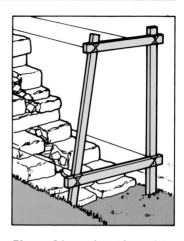

Above: *A batter frame is used to set the tilt of the wall.*

Above: *Build the wall against the bank topped with coping stones.*

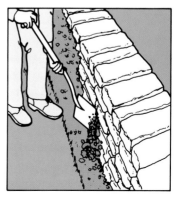

Above: *As you build, back-fill with subsoil, packed lightly.*

23

There's a vast selection of fencing types to choose from—whether it's a simple post-and-rail type to stake out your front garden boundary, a peep-proof woven fence in pre-made panels, or a closeboard version to provide a windbreak for the patio. Whatever the style of fence, they all have one thing in common —the humble post. Fixing can be as simple as digging a hole in the ground.

The basis of any fence is a stout vertical post to which the fence itself is attached. The post must be fixed firmly in the ground, and be able to withstand the brunt of the wind and effects of inclement weather. Concrete, durable and sturdy, is often used for posts, but timber is the most versatile material—it takes screws or nails well, can be sawn, drilled, and is fairly lightweight and easy to handle— despite being prone to rot.

TREATING THE POSTS

There's no way you can prevent decay, but you can curtail its progress by treating the timber with preservative re-applied every other year. Timber posts should be made from oak or chestnut for superior durability, but ask for 'tanalized' timber that has been impregnated with preservative. With untreated timber, brushing or spraying on preservative isn't enough to protect it: the ends of the posts should be soaked in fluid overnight. Stand them in a bucket containing the preservative and brush the liquid up their length frequently so it soaks in, especially the part to be set in the ground.

The most vulnerable part of the post is the end grain. Stop rainwater from settling and soaking into the top by sawing a single or double bevel, or attach a pre-made wood cap or a hood of lead, zinc or bituminous roofing felt turned down the sides and fixed with galvanized nails.

ARRANGING THE POSTS

Most fence posts are spaced out at 6ft (2m) intervals and if you're replacing an old fence run you'll be faced with removing the concrete collars used to secure the original posts. This is laborious, so begin the new run with a narrow section, so the new posts don't align with the old ones. Use stringlines and pegs to mark out the fence run.

It's likely that the first post in the run will have to be attached to the house wall. It should be about 24in (600mm) shorter than the other posts, as it won't be sunk in the ground. Drill holes through the post to take ¼in (6mm) expanding bolts— three if the post is over 5ft (1·5m) high; two otherwise—and counter-sink the heads so the edge of the panel will fit flush to the side. Hold the post in position and mark the wall, drill holes for the bolts, then attach the post.

If the fence run is long, hire a post hole-borer to dig the holes. Drive the blades into the ground then turn the

Above: *Wedge each fence post in a hole dug large enough to accommodate a hardcore base, to provide good drainage.*

Above: *Closeboard fencing makes a rigid screen and windbreak.*

handle at the top of the shank and press down; once the blades are buried, lift out the borer to remove the earth. The holes should be about 24in (600mm) deep for a tall fence (over 4ft/1·2m high), or 18in (450mm) for a smaller one. Dig an extra 6in (150mm) to accommodate a base of hardcore for drainage.

Set the first post in its hole and wedge it upright: check with a spirit level held against two adjacent sides. Position the next post along, prop it vertically then span between the two with a straight-edged plank. Place the spirit level on top to check that the posts are horizontal. Prepare a fairly dry concrete mix of 1 part cement: four parts all-in aggregate (or use a dry mix intended for fencing) and shovel it into the holes. Tamp down the concrete to dispel air pockets then round off the top so that water won't lie. Leave the concrete to harden for a few days before attaching the fencing.

Above: *After ensuring that each post is level, shovel concrete into the hole, tamp it down, and round off the surface with a trowel.*

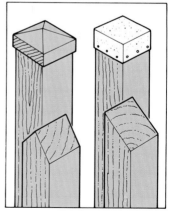

Above: *Protect post tops with proprietary caps, lead, zinc or felt covers or by cutting double or single bevels so rain runs off.*

For a sturdy boundary screen or simply a means of barring a neighbour's dog, panel or closeboard fences offer the best choice—they can be erected to numerous heights, clad in various ways and adapted to suit any space in the garden.

PREFABRICATED FENCING

The cheapest form of fence to provide low demarcation or total screening is the panel fence, notably the woven design. Panels are made in standard sizes: 6ft (1·8m) wide, and in 2, 3, 4, 5 and 6ft (600, 900, 1,200, 1,500, and 1,800mm) heights. A panel comprises thin pine or larch slats woven in basketweave around vertical battens and mounted in a softwood frame.

Wavy-edged panels have a more rustic appearance; they're made from thin wavy-edged pine or larch planks held within a softwood frame.

Panels are usually held between the posts by fixing through their outer frame with galvanized nails.

MADE-TO-MEASURE FENCING

Closeboard fencing is constructed from separate components on site to fit a particular space (prefabricated versions are available, though only rarely). More costly than panel fencing, closeboard fencing provides a more rigid, durable screen in the same sizes

The fence consists of two or three horizontal arris rails (depending on height) mortised into the posts and clad with vertical hardwood or softwood feather-edged boards. The boards are between 4 and 6in (100 and 150mm) wide and have one edge thinner than the other; they're nailed to the rails in overlapping fashion for a solid face. A horizontal gravel board is nailed to cleats, at the base of the posts: the boards rest on

its top edge, its purpose to stop damp rotting the boards.

Horizontal closeboard fencing is an alternative: the boards are nailed directly to the posts.

ATTACHING PANELS

Prefabricated panels are fixed to the posts using 3in (75mm) galvanized nails. First drill pilot holes through the side frames using an ⅛in (3mm) twist bit to avoid splitting the wood as they're driven in. Lift the panel between the posts and set on bricks so it's clear of the ground to prevent rot setting in. Nail the frame to the posts.

As an alternative to direct nailing, and where you're likely

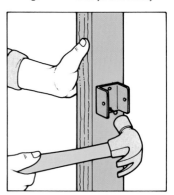

Top: *Nail a galvanized metal fixing-bracket to the post.*
Above: *Slot in the fence panel, then secure through the bracket.*

to want to remove the panels in the future for maintenance, attach two galvanized metal U-shaped brackets to the posts, slot in the panels and secure with rust-proof screws.

FITTING ARRIS RAILS

The triangular-section rails for closeboard fencing are usually bevelled at each end to fit slots in the posts (which you buy ready-mortised) by rough-sawing then smoothing with a planer file.

It's vital that the post slots are aligned—check with a stringline and line level—so you may prefer to use special arris rail brackets. First nail the brackets—angled galvanized metal strips with splayed ends for fixing to the posts—to the rails, position between the posts and secure with nails.

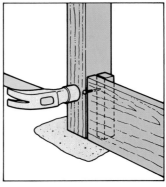

SECURING THE BOARDS

Before you fix the feather-edge boards, attach the gravel board to the posts at the base. Nail small softwood cleats to the posts near ground level. Cut 6 x 1in (150 x 25mm) gravel boards to fit between posts and nail to the cleats so they're flush with the posts and set perfectly horizontal.

Stand the first feather-edged board on the gravel board and butt its thick edge up to the post. Secure with 2in (50mm) galvanized nails to the arris rails. Position the second board so its thick edge overlaps the thin edge of the first board by ½in (12mm) and drive nails into the rails through both boards.

Proceed along the fence fixing boards, and checking that each one is vertical by holding a spirit level against it. Make a simple gauge from scrap timber with a notch the width of the board overlaps; use it to ensure consistent spacing. Reverse the last board so that its thick edge abuts the opposite post. Nail a bevelled coping strip on top.

Top: *Fix an arris rail by nailing on a splayed-end metal bracket.*
Centre: *Nail gravel boards to cleats fixed to the posts.*
Above: *Nail on the boards using a notched gauge for even spacing.*

For utilitarian fencing—to pen in animals, surround the vegetable plot or serve as a practical demarcation line—choose a simple post and wire fence. If your requirements are more decorative, however, picket types may fit the bill.

WIRE MESH FENCING

Open-mesh fencing is sold in rolls, commonly containing 33, 82, and 164ft (10, 25 and 50m) in heights from 12in (300mm) to 6ft (1.8m). The mesh itself may be ⅜ to 4in (10 to 100mm) in size. Welded and decorative versions are also made, and some types are plastic-coated for protection against rust (coloured green to blend with the garden).

The mesh is usually attached to ⅛in (3mm) galvanized steel posts to prevent it sagging—you'll need two lines for a fence under 4ft (1·2m) high and three for a taller one. You can, however, attach the mesh to timber posts. The end posts should be fitted with diagonal braces on the inner side to counteract the tension of the wire, which is stretched between straining bolts.

Fix the posts as for other fences. Screw eyebolts into the end posts and stretch the line wires between them. Retain against the intermediate posts with wire staples.

Staple one end of the mesh to an end post (or fix a straining bar to the eyebolts) then unroll it along the length of the fence, pull taut and attach to the line wires with tying wire. Stretch the mesh tight using the straining bolts.

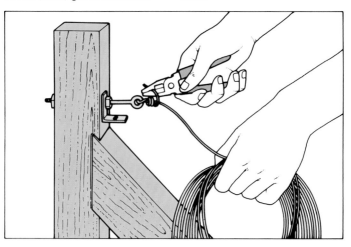

Above: *Wire mesh fencing can be attached between timber or metal posts; fix straining eyebolts at each end, top and bottom (in this case inserted in pre-drilled holes in the posts) then attach the line wires, winding them to secure using pliers. Stretch across to the opposite end post.*
Right: *Bolt a straining bar to the eyebolt's brackets, unroll the mesh, then tighten the straining eyebolts to stretch taut.*

SPLIT CHESTNUT PALINGS

More decorative, but just as functional, split chestnut paling comes in rolls about 30ft (9m) long and from 3ft (900mm) to 6ft (1·8m) in height. It comprises cleft chestnut stakes linked top and bottom to galvanized wire. The roll is stapled to softwood posts or chestnut poles driven into the ground at regular intervals. End posts should be 4in sq (100m sq), braced with struts; intermediate posts can be 3in sq (75mm sq) section.

PICKET FENCING

Popularly used as front garden fencing no higher than about 4ft (1·2m), picket is a type of closeboard structure, although the vertical boards (which are usually rounded or pointed at the top) are spaced apart about 3in (75mm). Kit versions are available using metal brackets for easy assembly.

Above: *Woven fencing can be bought in prefabricated panels.*

Easy to erect by nailing to the posts, it blends well with plants.

Above: *Closeboarded fences offer maximum privacy and are strong, too. They come in various designs,*

with horizontal or vertical boards, laid flush or feathered, as in these panels bolted to concrete posts.

A screen of timber trellis is a simple way to conceal a compost heap or rubbish bins, and provides an excellent base for training climbing plants. Prefabricated trellises are available but you may find the range of sizes limiting; making your own is easy using only a tenon saw, hammer and chisel.

DIAMOND TRELLIS

To construct a lightweight diamond trellis for fixing to the top of a fence or wall, first draw out the area you want to fill as a square or rectangle on the ground. Cut pieces of 1 x ¼in (25 x 6mm) softwood to length and lay them diagonally across the marked-out area, parallel to each other and space about 2-3in (50-75mm) apart.

Cut more strips to length and lay them diagonally opposite to, and across, the first batch. Pin the slats together at each intersection using ½in (12mm) tacks. Turn the lattice arrangement over and tap the ends of the tacks to bend them slightly and prevent the strips pulling apart. Nail to a thin wooden frame.

Below left: *Square trellis made with cross halving joints.*
Below: *Thin diamond latticework.*

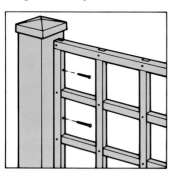
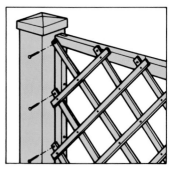

Above: *Tough square trellis is used as a boundary without making* a solid barrier that would blot out light and welcome breezes.

JOINTED TRELLIS

For a sturdier trellis up to 6ft
(1·8m) square and freestanding,
use 1in sq (25mm sq) timber,
assembled with cross-halving
joints for strengh—they restore the
wood's original thickness (and
strength). Cut the piece to length,
place on a flat surface side by
side with ends aligned,
and wrap adhesive tape around
them to hold them together.
Decide on the size of squares
you want and mark off the lengths;
allow the thickness of the timber
at each point (including the
ends for an outer frame member).
So that the joints are perfectly

square, mark across all strips
against a try square.

Remove the tape from the
strips, and continue the cutting
lines down their sides. Set a
marking gauge to ½in (12mm)
and scribe down each side
of the strips, between the pencil
lines to give the joint depth.
Tape the strips together again,
joints aligned. Saw down the
width lines to the thickness lines
with a tenon saw, then release the
strips. Place each strip on a piece
of scrap timber, and, using a 1in
(25mm) chisel, chop to the
gauged line bit by bit.

Assemble the trellis on a flat
surface by piecing together the
joints, using PVA glue on the
meeting faces. Reinforce each
joint by driving in a 1in (25mm)
galvanized nail.

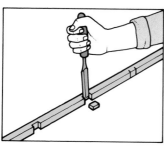

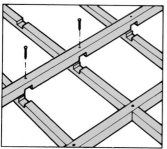

Above: *A strip of square trellis
fixed atop a fence gives extra
height to the boundary plus a
frame for growing climbers.*
Top left: *To make jointed trellis,
cut enough lengths of 1in sq
(25mm sq) timber, bunch them
together and mark all the joints.*
Centre left: *Mark the joint
depths with a marking gauge set
to half the wood thickness, then
chop out the waste with a chisel.*
Bottom left: *Assemble the cross-
halving joints with PVA glue and
1in (25mm) galvanized nails,
restoring the wood's thickness.*

SCREEN-BLOCK WALLS

If you'd like to shield your garden or patio from onlookers, but don't want to obliterate daylight and welcome cool breezes with a solid wall or fence, build a screen from pierced concrete blocks.

CHOOSING BLOCKS

Screen blocks are moulded from white concrete in 12in (300mm) squares, 4in (100mm) thick and pierced with geometric patterns —some are contained within a single block; others require several blocks to make a design. Solid blocks with a moulded pattern are also available—these

are ideal for breaking up an expanse of pierced blocks.

Blocks are laid in 'stack bond' —one on top of the other—but because there is no overlap between courses, the wall isn't intrinsically strong. Blocks cannot be cut and there are no half sizes, so your wall must be a number of whole blocks high and long.

BUILDING PIERS

To support the wall at intervals, build piers using hollow 8in (200mm) cubes called 'pilasters'. These incorporate slots to take the screen blocks. There are

Above: *Concrete screen-block walls come in a wide range of different designs and finishes.*

Their bold, geometric patterns blend well with the clean modern lines of patios like this one.

three types: with one slot for a stopped end; with slots on two opposite sides for an intermediate pier; with slots on two adjacent sides for a corner.

Where the wall is over about 6ft (1·8m) high and has piers at no more than 10ft (3m) intervals, the piers must be reinforced. Angle iron 2 x 2in (50 x 50mm) in section should be wire-tied to rods of ⅜in (10mm) mild steel, bent at right-angles and set in the foundation slab so that 12in (300mm) protrudes. The pilasters are slotted on and the cavities filled with a sloppy concrete mix.

To build the pier, prepare a mortar mix of 1 part masonry cement: 5 parts builder's sand, and trowel a bed on the foundation slab. Position the first pilaster squarely, tap level and remove excess mortar. Build three pilasters, then check the vertical level of the pier on two adjacent faces with a spirit level. Now build a second pier to this height: dry-lay the blocks with finger-width gaps between them to serve as joints for setting the piers the correct distance apart.

LAYING THE BLOCKS

Trowel a screed of mortar on the foundation slab running from the first pier about four block-widths long. Butter one edge of a block with mortar. Furrow the mortar, then position the block, buttered edge in the pilaster slot. Tap the block down with the handle of your trowel then scrape off excess mortar. Butter the outer edge of the block. Butt up the second block, tap down and check the level across both.

Lay two more blocks at the second pier, then stretch strings and pins between the blocks as a guide to laying the remainder of the course. Build up courses, extending the piers as necessary. Check with your spirit level that the blocks are horizontal and

flat across their faces—hold the level diagonally across to check for bowing.

Use corner pilasters to turn the wall at right-angles and build the second leaf in the same way. On a long wall, form a running pier and embed galvanized metal mesh in the horizontal mortar joints between the blocks to prevent the vertical joints from tearing open.

Complete the wall by bedding pilaster cappings on the piers and bevelled copings on the blocks. Point the joints by running a piece of hosepipe along to give a gentle rounded profile.

Above: *A low brick wall makes an ideal base for a classical patterned screen-block wall.*
Top: *A screen-block effect can be achieved in a brick wall by leaving gaps between bricks, honeycomb fashion.*

MAKING A GATE

A gate may confine children and pets safely to the garden or simply provide an attractive entrance to your property. Ready-made gates are available in various styles, but making one to your own design is quite straightforward.

HOW THE FRAME IS MADE

With a rigid basic frame, you can add the cladding you prefer —a vertical, horizontal or diagonal arrangement of boards or an airy slatted effect. Most of a gate's weight is supported on the hinge side, so the frame must be stout to withstand constant use without sagging. Hardwood is preferable for its weathering properties, but as it is also very costly, you may want to opt for planned (PAR) softwood. You

will need sufficient 4 x 1½in (100 x 40mm) timber for the stiles (uprights)—length depends on how high you want the gate to be. The top and bottom rails are of 3 x 1½in (75 x 40mm) timber. You'll also need a diagonal brace of 4 x ¾in (100 x 19mm) timber. Sizes of planed timber are nominal, so actual dimensions may be as much as ¼in (6mm) smaller all round.

Below: *The gate comprises an outer frame of 4 x 1½in (100 x 40mm) timber stiles; 3 x 1½in (75 x 40mm) top and bottom rails, mortise-and-tenoned for strength. The cladding—tongued-and-grooved boarding or slats—is nailed to an inner ½in sq (12mm sq) frame to which is screwed a diagonal brace of 4 x ¾in (100 x 19mm) timber.*

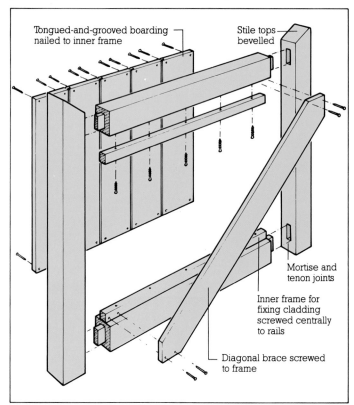

Tongued-and-grooved boarding nailed to inner frame

Stile tops bevelled

Mortise and tenon joints

Inner frame for fixing cladding screwed centrally to rails

Diagonal brace screwed to frame

ASSEMBLING THE FRAME

The frame is assembled using mortise and tenon joints: to mark out the joints, cut the pieces to length using a tenon saw. Lie a cross rail (to be tenoned) on a stile (to be mortised) and mark the tenon length—the tenons are 'stub' types, which don't protrude completely through the mortises; make them short of the stile by about ¾in (19mm). Square the mark around all four sides of the tenon piece by scoring across with a trimming knife against a try square. Set a mortise gauge—this has two pins instead of a marking gauge's single one—to ½in (12mm), the thickness of the tenon. With the rail set upright in a vice, use the gauge to score twin lines down the sides and across the end of the timber, stopping at the length marks you have just made.

Repeat the marking out procedure on the other end of the rail, then for both ends of the lower cross rail. Cross-hatch the waste areas in pencil, then cut the tenons.

To cut the tenons, clamp the rail at a 45° angle in a vice, then saw down the waste side of the gauge lines with a tenon saw, held horizontally. When you near the tenon length-mark, reverse the rail in the vice and saw down from the other corner. Set the piece upright and sawn down the triangle of waste remaining. Repeat for the other side of the tenon.

Hold or clamp the rail flat and cut away each of the tenon's face shoulders by sawing across the grain along the scribed lines. Repeat for the other rail.

To make the mortise into which the tenon slots, first square around the stiles 6in (150mm) from one end (the top) and 1in (25mm) from the other. Lay the stiles flat and rest the tenon on top, aligned with the squared lines. Mark the width of the tenon on the stiles, square it across

with a knife against a try square, then use the mortise gauge (set as before) to scribe between the width lines to give the mortise's width.

Measure off the length of the tenon on a ½in (12mm) diameter auger bit and wrap a piece of adhesive tape round it at this point, as a guide to drilling to the correct depth. Clamp the stile horizontally in a vice and drill closely-spaced holes as far as the tape, within the marked out mortise. The drilling removes the bulk of the mortise: use a ½in (12mm) mortise chisel to chop away the remaining waste, forming a square-sided slot. Repeat for the other end of the stile, then do likewise on the opposite stile.

Before assembling the joints, mark and cut a bevel on the top of each stile, from the outer edge sloping down to within about ½in (12mm) of the cross rail.

Clean all the joints by sanding then apply PVA adhesive to the tenon's shoulders. Assemble the frame by slotting the glued tenons into the mortises. Use two sash cramps to clamp the frame squarely and securely until the glue is dry. Locate the cramps directly over the joints and check that the internal angle of the frame is square, using a try square. Wipe off any smears of glue before it dries.

The gate frame is complete with the addition of a diagonal brace and an inner frame to which the cladding can be attached. To make the inner frame, cut four pieces of ½in sq (12mm sq) wood to fit within the outer frame. Attach to the frame, butt-jointing the corners, with 1in (25mm) brass screws—the inner frame should be positioned ¾in (19mm) from the inner face of the gate (mark this position using a marking gauge set to this dimension). The diagonal brace is screwed to the inner frame, and lies flush with the inner face of the gate. Hold the timber in place on the frame and mark where it needs to be cut to fit into the top (opening side) corner and the bottom (hinged side) corner. Cut it to size, then attach it with rust-proof screws.

FITTING THE CLADDING

The cladding for a solid gate can be of 4 x ½in (100 x 12mm) tongued-and-grooved boards: slot together the number of boards you need (trim the outer ones down their length to fit) and fix within the frame by pinning to the inner frame and to the diagonal cross-brace.

For spaced slats, use 4, 3 or 2in (100, 75, 50mm) timber ¾in (19mm) thick—or a mixture of each—and nail within the outer frame to the inner one.

For palings protruding from the top of the frame, substitute the top cross rail for a thinner one of 4 x ¾in (100 x 19mm) softwood and attach the palings to it, the brace and inner frame on the lower rail.

SETTING THE POSTS

If you are fitting the gate on existing concrete, brick or stone piers, there will probably be projecting hinge pins set within the structure, onto which you can drop the new gate fixings. In this instance, use bolt-on double-strap hinges: these metal flanges have an integral slot for the hinge pins, and bolt to each side of the cross rails.

Versions for timber posts are made, too. If you are fitting new posts, there are other options: T-hinges (screw-on strap for the gate attached to a screw-on flap for the post); hook-and-band types (separate hook for the post and screw-on strap for the gate); or reversible hinges (pin housed in two screw-on cups, which can be used either way up).

If you are fitting the gate between existing posts, you will have had the chance to tailor it to fit the space. If the gate and post are new installations, either build new piers (see page 18) or set timber posts in the ground. For posts, use 4in sq (100mm sq) planed, preservative-treated

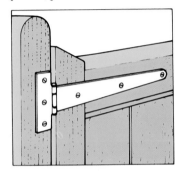

Above: *Pre-drill the fixing holes to fix this T-hinge to the gate.*

Above: *Position the latch accurately and screw it firmly to the gate.*

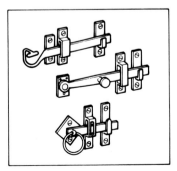

Above: *Various designs of lever-operated latch are available.*

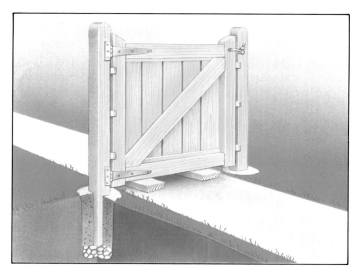

Above: *The finished gate, set in hardcore and concrete foundations.*

timber; bevel or round off the tops so rainwater won't soak in and cause rot.

To set the posts the correct distance apart, lay them on the ground with the gate between them. Allow a gap of ¼in (6mm) between the stiles and posts, then cut a length of batten to fit between the posts and use as a gauge to help you position them accurately.

Using the rod as a positioning guide, dig the post holes deep enough to allow a clearance of 2in (50mm) underneath the gate —there should be 18in (450mm) below ground level. Set the posts on a firm base of 4in (100mm) hardcore, then pack round them with more rubble. Check that the posts are aligned with the boundary and set them vertically using a spirit level on adjacent faces. Support the posts temporarily with struts wedged to stakes, place a straight-edge and spirit level across their tops to make sure they are level, then pour concrete into the holes, compact and leave to set.

HANGING THE GATE

Stand the gate between the posts on offcuts of timber and pack out the sides with offcuts, ensuring there is ¼in (6mm) clearance at each side. Place your spirit level on the top cross-rail to make sure the gate is level.

With T-hinges, hold the fitting against the gate and post and mark through the screw fixing holes. Remove the hinges, drill pilot hole for the screws, then attach the hinges to the gate. Offer up the gate again and screw the hinge flaps to the post.

With strap-type hinges, fix the strap part to the gate first, using the screws and bolts provided. Set the gate in the open position, mark the screw holes for the hook on the post, then screw it in place. With reversible hinges, fix the bottom cup first, position the gate, then mark and fix the upper cup retaining the gate.

Most latches comprise a lever, operated by pushing one end down or lifting a bar, and a keep-plate. Automatic latches have a thumb-operated lever which releases the bar. With the gate closed, hold the latch mechanism in place and mark its fixing holes, then screw it into place and test its operation.

SURFACE MATERIALS

A path is primarily practical, enabling you to get from A to B without compacting the earth or having to walk across wet grass. If you prefer a less active role in gardening, consider constructing a patio, where you can loll in comfort while others work. Whether you want access through the plot or a surface that gets you nowhere, you'll find there's a vast selection of suitable materials.

CHOOSING MATERIALS

Consider the ambience you want to create in your garden when shopping for suitable materials for a path and patio, but bear in mind the practicalities, too. Also, after reading through this section, look at the section on planning the route your path is to take (page 40).

CAST CONCRETE

Cast concrete is tough and adaptable, but also inherently plain and stark; however, it can be moulded to the shape you want—even curves—and its durability is hard to beat. Major drawbacks are that frost can crack it and that it takes a long time to weather in. However, you can impress on it a non-slip finish—vital in a sloping garden.

SLABS

Slabs, cast in concrete, offer a variety of colours (reds, greens, greys, yellows and buff tones) and geometric shapes (squares, rectangles, hexagons, octagons and circles).

Slabs are typically 2in (50mm) thick and come in various sizes, commonly 18 x 18in (450 x 450mm) and half sizes. Other shapes range from about 9in sq (225mm sq) to about 27 x 18in (675 x 450mm). Lay a combination of sizes and shapes for decorative effect. Various finishes are made: smooth, with a non-slip surface;

Above: *The slightly uneven surface of a brick path ensures a firm foothold, even in wet weather, and gives a gentle, rustic effect.*

textured, with exposed aggregate; riven, resembling split stone; and patterned, with a brick, tile or cobblestone effect.

Broken concrete slabs are sold (by the square yard or ton) as crazy paving, in many shapes, sizes and colours. Loose stones can be a chore to lay over a wide area, and they can also be a trip hazard if uneven.

PAVERS

Small-scale paving blocks moulded from concrete to resemble bricks can be used to create a surface that blends with either a plain or a well-established plot and, laid with the patterns intended—herring-bone or basketweave, for example —will enhance the scheme.

Various colours are available, from subtle brick-reds and

browns to light sandy tones, greys and burnt-brick effects. Blocks may be textured for authenticity, and some incorporate neat bevels around the top edge to accentuate their shape. The blocks are roughly brick-sized—8 x 4in (200 x 100mm) and 1½ or 2½in (35 or 65mm) thick. Shaped, interlocking versions are also made—popularly S- and Y-shaped —to create a complex surface.

Old bricks are an alternative to blocks, although you must use ones suitable for paving— some are too porous.

FEATURE AREAS

Acres of concrete or slabs can look harsh, and smaller-scale materials can help to break up the plainness. Cobbles—small rounded stones—set in concrete can be used to replace individual slabs. Gravel, perhaps as an edging strip, offers the same contrast and, if placed over soil, can even be used as a medium for growing plants.

Above: *Shaped interlocking blocks are easily laid on a sand base.*
Centre: *Set pebbles in a concrete path for interesting varied texture.*

LAYING A PATH

PLANNING ROUTES

Whatever material you have chosen for your path, planning out its route through the garden is your priority. If the path is purely a means of connecting the various areas of the garden, incorporate curves to avoid segmenting the plot. Take into account the lie of the land: if the ground slopes towards the house or outbuildings, remember that rainwater will be able to flow uninterrupted to the walls rather than soaking into the ground as it normally would.

Draw a sketch plan and a side elevation of your garden so you can take into account these points when planning the path.

Above: *This gently curving path of coloured concrete slabs is designed to provide a welcoming invitation to the house.*

ARRANGING THE FORMWORK

A concrete path is a good choice where you want a smooth, flat surface for transporting items by barrow; you can also use the concrete as a base for other materials, such as small-scale pavers, which benefit from solid foundations, especially if the ground is soft.

Set the wet mix within timber formwork to mould and retain it until hard, in the same way as when making slab or strip foundations. Plot out the path with strings and pegs, set datums from which to position stakes, then nail the form boards to them. On a flat site, incorporate a drainage cross-fall running to one side of a path.

For a long path, divide the length into bays about 10ft (3m) long to prevent the concrete from cracking due to expansion and contraction: cut a strip of ½in (12mm) softwood the depth of the concrete to fit between the side forms and temporarily secure it with stakes (thoroughly treat the strip with preservative before fitting: it is to remain in the slab, where it will be exposed to damp and resultant rot).

Cast the concrete in one bay on a layer of well-rammed hard-core topped with a blinding layer of building sand to fill any voids. Tamp the mix to dispel air bubbles then, when the concrete has almost set, remove the stakes holding the expansion strip and add the concrete to the adjoining bay, sandwiching it in place.

You can make a curved path by making a number of saw cuts across the form boards at 5in (125mm) intervals, enough to enable the timber to be bent; you will need to fix extra stakes to prevent the boards from springing back straight again.

Above: *Precast concrete slabs, made to simulate natural stone are laid in an interesting pattern to create a solid, attractive path allowing safe access to the garden shed no matter what the weather. The bold, functional lines of the paving slabs are softened by allowing the flowers in the border to spill out onto them. Concrete slabs can be laid on a levelled base of sand or in mortar, if they are to take heavy traffic. They are hardwearing and will mellow with age.*

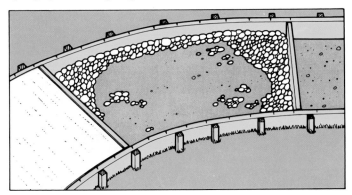

Above: *For a curved path in concrete, make a number of saw cuts across the formboards at 5in (125mm) intervals so you can bend the timber as required. More stakes are needed in order to retain the boards in their curves without their springing straight.*

Above: *Broken bricks and stones, rammed down over firmed subsoil,* *form a sturdy, well-draining foundation for flexible pavers.*

Above: *The hardcore layer should then be covered with a 1½in* *(40mm) layer of coarse sand, levelled with a straight-edge.*

LAYING FLEXIBLE PAVERS

Concrete block pavers are bedded dry, without mortar, on a sand bed. The joy of 'flexible' paving is that individual blocks can easily be removed, if necessary in the future, for repairs to underground drainpipes, to correct land drainage faults—or simply if you feel like altering the original pattern. Dry-laying also provides a quick way to pave a large area such as a patio.

The best foundation for flexible paving comprises well-rammed hardcore over firmed subsoil—remove as many weeds as you can before laying. Treat the ground with weedkiller to reach dormant seeds, as they will grow up between the blocks.

LAYING IN PATTERNS

You can lay the block pavers in numerous patterns, typically running bond, herringbone, basketweave or parquet. Plan out the design on paper first so that you can count up the exact number of whole and cut blocks you will need, and also to determine the exact size of the area you are laying.

EDGE RESTRAINTS

Edge restraints are necessary to prevent the pavers from

Above: *Lay a patio of concrete slabs with a kerb to stop them spreading.*

Above: *The end result—an attractive tough and durable patio.*

spreading: you can but the blocks up to house or other walls—taking care to set them sufficiently below the DPC—and rig up supports elsewhere using 5 x 2in (125 x 50mm) precast concrete kerbstones. Set the stones in a trench, bedded in concrete.

Less durable, but also less conspicuous than kerbstones, timber planks (well-treated against rot) can be nailed to stakes at the perimeter of the proposed patio.

BEDDING SAND

Spread the sand onto the sub-base between the restraints, and rake it to a rough level. With the base covered, use a straight-edged plank to draw the sand level and smooth to about 2½in (60mm) deep. Don't forget to include a drainage fall (away from the house) by levelling the sand bed using a shim of wood under one end of the spirit level.

PLACING THE BLOCKS

Starting at an edge restraint, position the first blocks on the sand bed in your chosen pattern —leave gaps for the cut blocks, to be filled in later. Continue to place the blocks in an easily manageable area, then place a plank over them to spread your load, move forward onto it, and lay more blocks. Progress across the site in this way.

When you have laid the whole blocks, return to the starting point and cut blocks to fit the gaps. If you have a large area to fill, hire a hydraulic stone splitter, which tackles the cutting quickly and accurately. If you are cutting by hand, score the block all round by tapping with a bolster chisel, then place on a firm, level surface and strike the line hard with a club hammer and bolster to break the block. Position the cut side against the edge restraint.

COMPACTING THE SURFACE

Spread a layer of sand over the surface and brush it into the joints between blocks. On a large area, hire a motorized plate compactor (fitted with a rubber sole plate; or use it over an old piece of carpet to protect the blocks). Run the plate compactor over the paving to vibrate each block firmly into the sand bed. Add more sand and brush it into the joints.

You can compact the blocks by hand if you wish: place a stout length of timber over several blocks and bash it with a club hammer rhythmically and check for consistent level frequently.

SURFACING A DRIVEWAY

A driveway receives a lot of hard wear, so it is hardly surprising that eventually it becomes cracked, potholed and shabby. But you needn't resort to digging it up and starting again—durable asphalt and coloured stone chippings can be used to revitalize a poor surface.

TYPES OF SURFACE DRESSING

Three types of surface dressing are commonly available for applying to an old drive: one comprises a scattering of white, pink, green or amber stone chippings stuck to a coating of thick bitumen emulsion, which binds the stones and does not raise the surface unduly.

The second method involves spreading a proprietary asphalt over the base. The surface—which may be green, red or black—is then rolled and left to harden.

The third method is similar, but uses a surface dressing of another asphalt, applied hot. Chippings can then be scattered over the surface to give a loose-grained finish.

Below: *Pink asphalt, laid cold with white chippings rolled in to form a random pattern, makes a durable and attractive driveway. The colour blends well with the brickwork of the house and wall.*

POURING LIQUID BITUMEN

Make good cracks, crumbled edges and large potholes with dry-mixed concrete, allow to dry, then brush the surface to remove debris. Transfer some bitumen from its large drum to a 1 gal (5 litre) watering can with the rose removed. Working in a small, easily-maneagable area (the watering can should hold enough to cope with about 5sq yd/4sq m), pour the liquid onto the surface and spread it out with an old broom to form a fine film. Scatter on chippings: allow about 1cu ft (50kg) per 7sq yd (6sq m). Fill any gaps, the roll the surface.

USING COLD ASPHALT

Allow about 2cwt (100kg) of cold asphalt per 4sq yd (3½sq m), giving ½in (12mm) thickness. Use it to fill any potholes before adding the top covering. Apply bitumen emulsion to concrete or loose material for a better bond. Allow it to set—it changes from brown to black in about twenty minutes—before tipping on the contents of the sacks. Rake out the material to about ¾in (19mm) thickness, then roll.

Scatter chippings thinly over the surface to break up the overall colour, or leave as it is. Roll again, tamping the edges.

APPLYING HOT ASPHALT

Hot asphalt can be obtained from specialist suppliers, and is delivered by tipper lorry, dumped on your prepared base and spread out flat, then rolled. Work quickly: asphalt sets as it cools.

If the drive abuts a lower level, set precast kerbstones in concrete to prevent the chippings from spilling over the edge. Use a wide rake—you can hire asphalt rakes and eight-pronged forks for loading the barrow—to spread out the asphalt to about 1½in (38mm) thickness. Turn the rake

over to smooth the asphalt.

When about a quarter of your area has been coated, scatter a few shovelfuls of chippings thinly over the surface, then use a motorized plate compactor to vibrate the surface flat. Where the drive joints the road or path, rake the asphalt thinner to avoid a ridge. When all the material is laid and vibrated, roll with a heavy-duty roller, then scatter more chippings over the drive, either to conceal the material, or to allow it to show through slightly.

Above: *Plain black asphalt is well suited to functional driveways whose appearance is not of prime importance.*

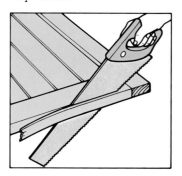

Above: *You will have to remove your garage door and saw a strip off the bottom so that it will open over the new drive surface.*

FREESTANDING STEPS

A flight of steps provides access to the various parts of a split-level or sloping garden and helps to visually link the separate elements. Freestanding steps rise from ground level to a higher, terraced level, such as a raised lawn or patio in a formal plot.

PLANNING THE STEPS

The initial stage in planning steps is to decide on their scale, using a sensible, safe formula: the steps should be uniform in size, neither too shallow nor too steep. For comfortable walking, the risers (vertical faces of the steps) should be between 4 and 7in (100 and 175mm) deep. The treads (on which you walk) should not be less than 12in (300mm) from front to back: ample to take the ball of your foot on descending without the back of your leg touching the step above. Treads should be 24in (600mm) wide for one person; 60in (1·5m) for two.

The tread should incorporate a 'nosing'—the front protruding beyond the riser by 1in (25mm) so that the shape of the step is defined in shadow. Calculate how many steps you will need by measuring the vertical height you

Top left: Build the first riser box and fill with hardcore.
Top right: Add the second riser box on top of the first.

Above left: Bed the slab treads on five dabs of mortar each.
Above right: Leave the finished steps for a few days before use.

want to scale and then dividing this figure by the height of a single riser.

Choosing materials depends on the effect you want. Free-standing steps suit a more formal scheme, so bricks are ideal for making risers (blocks with split stone faces would soften the effect). Slab treads give a flat, firm surface.

BUILDING THE RISERS

The steps are formed by building U-shaped retaining walls which make up the risers, butted up to the terrace you're scaling. Each 'box' is back-filled with hardcore and subsequent, smaller boxes built on top.

Make strip foundations for the bottom riser of a typical three- or four-step flight (a raft is needed for anything bulkier plus honeycomb intermediate walls under each riser). Set up string-lines to indicate the width and height of the first riser.

Dry-lay the bricks or blocks for the first riser (two courses are ample) to choose the best bonding arrangement: stretcher bond is the simplest, with cut units at the back of the riser. Lay the first course of bricks or blocks on a mortar screed, turning them header-on at the corners and running down to the terrace wall. Use your stringlines as a

Above: *These freestanding steps, made of coloured concrete blocks, form a simple yet elegant link between garden and patio.*

guide to laying accurately, and check for level frequently.

Allow the mortar to set partially, then tip shovelfuls of hardcore inside the box. Tamp it down with a sledgehammer. Raise the side strings to the second riser height and move the front ones back. Cover the hardcore with a blinding layer of sand to fill voids, then lay the second riser on top of the first.

When the mortar has set, add more hardcore, compact it and carry on building subsequent steps. As the courses rise, check with a gauge rod that joints are consistent; hold a spirit level across the sides to check for bowing. Point the joints with neat rounded profiles.

ADDING THE TREADS

The slabs should overhang the risers at the front and sides by about 1in (25mm). Bed them on the risers on either five dabs or a complete bed of mortar. Tap them down with the handle of your trowel so they slope slightly to the front for drainage. Point the joints between abutting slabs, and also where they meet the next riser.

CUT-IN STEPS

Where you want to provide access through a sloping garden, inconspicuous cut-in steps allow you to retain the overall profile of the ground by using the bank itself as their foundations.

PROVIDING FOOTINGS

A cut-in flight makes use of the structure of the bank as its main support, but you should include provision for concrete footings below the first riser, to prevent the flight from slipping downwards. The footings can be a simple strip of concrete about 3in (75mm) thick, laid on hardcore and twice as wide as the step.

CUTTING THE SHAPE

Before you plot out the shape of your cut-in steps, measure the vertical height of the slope you are scaling: drive in a peg at the top and a long cane at the base; tie string between the pegs and set it horizontal using a spirit level. Measure from the string to the base of the cane and divide the riser height into this dimension to tell you how many steps you will need. If the riser height (see previous page) will not divide into this, you may have to remodel the earth accordingly, using the cut-and-fill technique (see page 10).

Stretch strings between pegs down the length of the slope to indicate the sides of the flight, then arrange more across the flight: the strings should mark the position of the nosing of each tread, as a guide to laying the masonry accurately.

Cut out the rough shape of the steps using a spade, working from the top to the bottom of the bank so there is no risk of the excavation collapsing. Take care not to dislodge the nosing strings. With the flight planned out, firm the soil by tamping with a sledgehammer—beware of crumbling the edges, however.

Below: *Cut-in steps are ideal for blending in with an informal garden scheme to highlight attractive changes of level.*

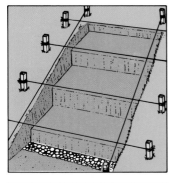

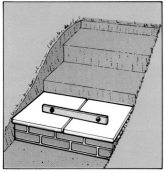

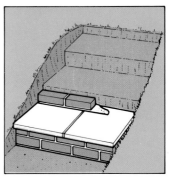

Top left: *Mark tread nosings; dig out rough shape of steps.*
Top right: *Build first riser and back-fill with hardcore.*

Above left: *Bed the treads on mortar with a fall to the front.*
Above right: *Build a second riser on the back of the first step.*

MAKING THE RISERS

Place hardcore at the first riser position and compact it thoroughly with a sledgehammer. Trowel on a fairly stiff mortar mix of 1 part cement : 5 parts sand, then lay the first course of blocks. Lay the second course on top, staggering the joints.

Check the level of the blockwork with a spirit level—the top front edge of the riser should run along the stringline—and tap down with the handle of your trowel to correct any irregularity, or pack out with more mortar. Check that the riser is square.

If there is a gap between the riser and the excavation, fill it with hardcore and compact it so it is flush with the top of the blocks. Shovel more hardcore

onto the first tread position and ram it down thoroughly. Place your spirit level on the step with a shim under the lower end, to the drainage fall.

LAYING THE TREADS

Bed down the slabs forming the first tread on a complete screed or five dabs of mortar and level them both crossways and front to back. Don't forget to allow a nosing of about 1in (25mm) projecting beyond the riser.

Lay the second riser block courses either on the back of the first tread slabs, or directly behind them.

Back-fill with hardcore and compact well, then place the next treads. Continue up the bank until the flight is complete.

PERGOLA

A pergola can be used to display a flowering climber or shade part of the patio. Attached to the house wall, it can conceal an ugly aspect or merely provide an intimate place to sit out on sunny days.

ATTACHING THE WALL PLATE

The rafters, supported at the house wall on a timber plate, are notched over a cross-piece at the outer edge, which itself slots into a notch in the post tops. All timber should be cut to size and shape, then treated with preservative.

The wall plate is of 4 x 2in (100 x 50mm) timber—length depends on how broad you want your pergola. Mark off the 1in (25mm) wide notch positions at 36in (900mm) intervals. Square lines around the timber at these marks against a try square. Set a marking gauge to half the timber thickness and scribe

Below: *A pergola attached to the house can be used to create a leafy bower for relaxing in the heat of the day.*

between the width lines to mark the depth of the notches.

Use a tenon saw to cut down the waste side of the width lines as far as the depth lines. Lie the plate on a flat surface and use a chisel to pare away the waste. With the notches cut, drill holes through the plate at 24in (600mm) intervals to take 165 x 16mm steel anchor bolts, using a 1in (25mm) flat bit. Offer up the plate to the wall, set horizontal using a spirit level, then mark the wall through the holes. Drill 4½in (12mm) deep holes for the fixings, using a 1½in (35mm) masonry bit.

Remove the outer shells from each of the anchor bolts, push them into the wall, then insert their bolts through the holes in the plate, locate in the wall and tighten with an adjustable wrench to secure the plate.

ERECTING THE POSTS

The posts are made from 4in sq (100mm sq) sawn softwood; they should reach from ground level to the base of the wall plate, but allow extra to be set in the

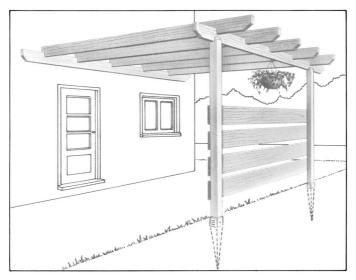

ground. Digging post holes is a chore, so use metal stake supports. Each one consists of a long spike with a square socket on top, into which the post is slotted and secured by nails. The spikes also protect the timber from rot. To fit a spike, slot an offcut of post in the socket and drive it into the ground. Then remove the offcut.

Before fitting the posts, cut 2in (50mm) deep notches, 2in (50mm) wide in their tops, to take the cross-rafter. Bevel the top corners so that rainwater will not settle there.

ATTACHING THE RAFTERS

Cut to length the cross-piece, which slots in the post notches, bevel the ends, then lift it into place and secure it by 'skew-nailing': drive the nails through the posts into the rail at an angle to prevent them working their way out. Cut the rafters to length and shape their ends. Cut notches about 24in (600mm) from the outer ends and slot them onto the cross-piece. Slot the house ends into the wall plate notches and secure them by skew-nailing.

Above: *This timber pergola consists of rafters resting on a wall plate and supported on a cross rafter, itself notched into stout posts sunk in the ground with metal spikes. An arrangement of planks between posts provides a degree of privacy when sitting out under the canopy, and is easily nailed in place.*

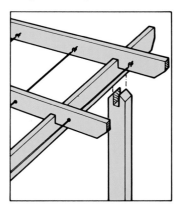

Above: *The rafters are notched to sit on the cross-piece, itself slotted into a notch in the post tops (bevelled to shed rain). Wires slotted through the rafters, retained by screw-eyes, provide a frame for climbers.*

A rustic garden arch can bring a touch of countryside charm to any garden. Freestanding, it can become a focal point of the plot, and a framework for the attentions of climbing plants; built into a run of fencing, between two lush hedges or even filling a gap in a brick wall, the arch can be an informal division between two areas.

DESIGNING YOUR ARCH

You don't have to follow the precise construction method shown here to duplicate this design—the versatility of rustic poles means that you can adapt the basic framework to create an individual structure. Keep the proportions of the arch within sensible bounds: if it is too tall it will dwarf all around it and its rigidity will be dwindled; if it is too narrow you will have difficulty passing through with a loaded wheelbarrow or other garden implements, without snagging clothes and skin. A height of about 8ft (2m) is reasonable and a width of 4ft (1·2m) sufficient.

As far as choice of timber is concerned, you have the option of rustic poles with or without the bark—there is little to sway you either way except aesthetic value. Size is a different matter, and the pole for the main frame-work should be about 3in (75mm) in diameter for rigidity; smaller diameter pole will suffice for the bracing struts and latticework. Buy the poles at a garden centre or timber yard.

CUTTING NOTCHES

Most of the components of the arch can be connected simply by nailing them together, but the larger frame members should be jointed to increase the surface contact area: simple notches, as shown below, are chopped in the poles and the flat areas formed are pieced together and secured with 4in (100mm)

galvanized wire nails.

Typical joints you will need to use include the halving joint, for poles that cross each other: mark the diameter of the poles on the meeting pieces and cut (using a coping saw) to half their depth; chisel out the waste and bring the poles together, restoring their original thickness.

Use the 'bird's-mouth' joint where a rail abuts a post: cut a V-shape in the post and a matching pointed end on the rail and slot it into the recess.

Connect two poles end to end with half-lap notches, slanted if the poles are to meet at a point. Rest rails on the tops of bird's-mouth-notched posts, or cut a notch in the underside of the rail and set it onto the square end of a post.

ASSEMBLING THE FRAME

Cut the main posts to length, allowing 18in (450mm) for sinking

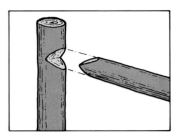

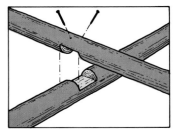

Top: *Cut a bird's-mouth joint where a cross rail abuts a post; skew-nail from top and bottom.*
Above: *A halving joint is ideal where poles cross; it restores the wood's original thickness.*

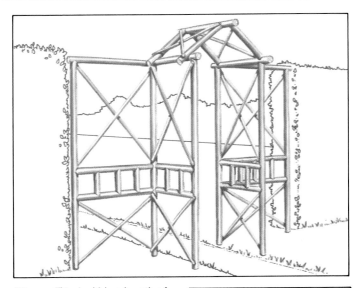

Above: *Fitted within a length of hedge or wall, a rustic arch can be constructed with side wings and adorned with beautiful climbing plants.*

in the ground. Lay them on the ground the correct distance apart. Position the cross-rails, braces and latticework where required, mark their joints and cut them. Assemble the side wings of the arch in the same way. Piece together the top frame, too, so that the prefabricated units can be assembled on site. Secure each joint by driving in nails dovetail fashion: at an angle to each other, so they cannot be withdrawn.

If you are using poles without bark, soak them in preservative for about 24 hours, paying particular attention to the cut ends and joints. Preservative will not penetrate timber with the bark left on so the best solution is to scorch the ends with a blowtorch to seal the pores. Nevertheless, it is a good idea to creosote the end to be set in the ground.

Dig holes in the ground for the posts, add hardcore and tamp down for a free-draining, firm surface, then set the side frames

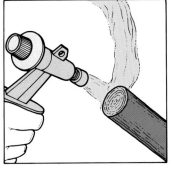

Above: *Seal the pores of the poles by scorching the cut ends with a blowtorch flame. Take care not to burn the poles.*

and wings in place (if the wings abut a wall or existing fence, screw them in place for extra rigidity). Prop the frames upright with battens; fill around them with coarse concrete—use dry-mixed ingredients ready-bagged for setting fence posts. When the concrete has fully hardened, position the arch top and secure with 4in (100mm) rust-proof screws inserted through pre-drilled clearance holes: the unit will be too flexible to permit nailing on the top.

TIMBER PLANTER

A raised planter brings blooms within comfortable reach without resorting to stooping, is the neat solution in a patio garden and a clever way to make a sloping plot accessible. This split-level timber structure looks at home in either an orderly or less contrived scheme—it is easy to build without complicated woodworking joints.

PLANTER FORMAT

The planter is basically a box to contain the earth, providing a neat growing area especially suited to a paved garden, where it prevents soil from spilling onto the stones. It can be constructed on flat ground, although its charm lies in its split-level arrangement.

The planter starts life as a mound of earth—either an existing bank or remodelled ground (see page 10)—which you enclose with the timber framework, then redistribute to fill the box shapes.

The timber is the sawn type, 3 x 2in (75 x 50mm) for the supporting posts; 6 x 2in (150 x 50mm) for the plank infill. Planks are simply stacked one on top of the other, retained by the posts and secured with galvanized nails. Treat all timber with preservative before use, preferably by soaking in a home-made bath of fluid for a few days for maximum protection.

Plot out the planter on graph paper first so that you can accurately determine the lengths of timber you will need to buy: purchase it in long lengths—it is sold in standard sizes up to 10ft (3m)—and cut it to size yourself for economy, using a panel saw.

SINKING THE POSTS

Mark out the site with strings and pegs before starting construction, then dig the post holes. It is vital that the posts are set firmly in the ground as they will have to hold back a considerable weight of soil, plus the planking. Set them about 24in (600mm) deep, resting on well-rammed hardcore (which provides a firm foundation and a free-draining base). Span between the posts with a straight-edged plank and spirit level to set them at the same level.

Hire a post-hole-borer to make the hole, or use metal post

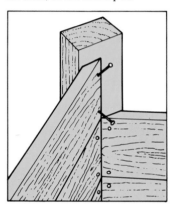

Above: *Where the planks abut the posts, secure them by skew-nailing. Drive nails in at opposite angles so they will not work loose.*

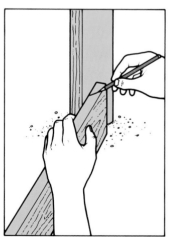

Above: *Mitre the ends of the planks so they fit flush with the back of the posts; use a circular saw with angled sole plate.*

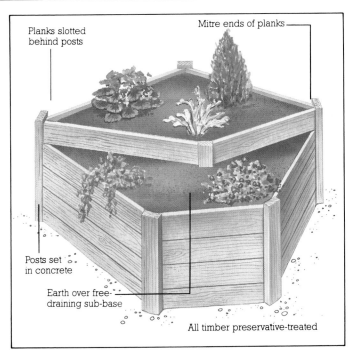

Planks slotted behind posts

Mitre ends of planks

Posts set in concrete

Earth over free-draining sub-base

All timber preservative-treated

Above: *The planter is made from 6 x 2in (150 x 50mm) planks held within a frame of 3 x 2in (75 x 50mm) posts. The design can* *be adapted to suit flat ground or a split-level garden; several tiers can be added and the basic shape altered to your preference.*

spikes to secure the uprights to save having to dig holes at all. Ensure the posts are set vertical so the planks can be attached perfectly squarely.

INSTALLING THE PLANKS

It is best to cut the planks accurately to length when the posts have been set: measure between the uprights for precise dimensions. The ends of the planks are mitred to fit flush against the backs of the posts. The best way to cut these is with a power circular saw (you can hire this), which has an adjustable sole plate. This enables you to set the angle of the blade to precisely that required for the mitre: hold the plank in place to mark this.

Position the lowest planks about 2in (50mm) below ground level to prevent soil from the planter leaching out onto the paving. Set them on a thin layer of gravel for drainage and use a spirit level to check that they are horizontal. Tap down or pack out the planks accordingly until they are level.

Secure the planks to the posts by skew-nailing, using two nails per plank. With the main box built, distribute the soil so that it is flat and about 1in (25mm) below the level of the planks to prevent it spilling over. Set a central post in the mound and fit a single plank between it and the longer back posts. Fill the top box with soil and spread flat.

Leave the nail to settle for a few weeks, then top up, if necessary, and plant out with shrubs as required, or install a garden pond (see page 60).

WINDOW BOX

If the view from your window is less than attractive, brighten it with this ingenious tiered window box. It is ideal for fixing below an upstairs or a downstairs window, and the plants can be tended from the window or from below via ladders.

Flat-dwellers need not be robbed of the pleasures of enjoying attractive blooms, so long as they've a handy window sill. But usually sills cannot cope with more than one trough or a row of pots: this hanging window box, however, makes full use of the wasted space below the sill—and beyond it, by actually extending the usable area into space.

The design is based around standard-sized plastic plant troughs: the top tier holds one trough; the lower tier holds two. There's no reason why you shouldn't extend the tiers to three or four—space below permitting—as the weight of the containers is distributed along sturdy wall battens and receives extra support from a pair of diagonal braces.

Whatever your plans, it is essential that you check first with your neighbours underneath you that your plans are acceptable. Make sure that your window box will not obscure their view, block off their light, or drip water on them.

Below: *The hanging window box allows easy access to the contents; the considerable weight is transmitted to the wall.*

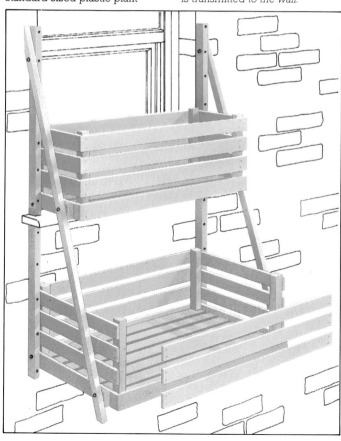

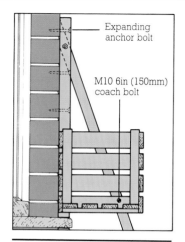

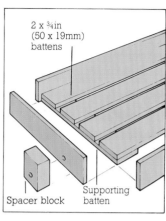

Above left: *The unit in section.*
Above: *Box-base construction.*

MAKING THE BOXES

The plant boxes themselves, which contain the troughs, are simple slatted structures: cut four corner posts per box, 12in (300mm) long, from rough-sawn timber 2in sq (50mm sq). To these posts nail slats of 2 x ¾in (50 x 19mm) planed softwood, leaving ¾in (19mm) gaps between each. Fix the long slats across the front and back posts, extending beyond the sides by ¾in (19mm); nail the shorter, front-to-back slats to the posts between the long slats.

The exact length and depth of the boxes depends on the size of troughs you're using. These come in a range of sizes, usually about 8in (200mm) across the base to fit on a standard sill, and between 12 and 36in (300 and 900mm) long to suit various sizes of windows. The trough needs to be about 4in (100mm) shorter than the window width to allow for the width of the slatted box.

The bases of the boxes are slatted, too, comprising 2 x ¾in (50 x 19mm) battens screwed (using 1in/25mm long rustproof screws) to supporting battens of timber of the same section. These are nailed to the outside faces of the vertical posts of the box sides. If you do not wish to use troughs, you can substitute plastic plant pots.

FITTING THE WALL BATTENS

The plant boxes are bolted to 2in sq (50mm sq) sawn softwood battens (using M10 6in/150mm long coach bolts, which are fastened vertically to the wall by expanding anchor bolts for maximum strengths. The battens run past each end of the sill (the top plant box rests on the sill and is secured to it) and extend just below the lower box and a short distance above the higher box. The boxes are fastened to the battens with M10 6in (150mm) long coach bolts driven through their base battens.

A pair of diagonal supporting struts span from the outer bottom corner of the lower plant box to the top of the vertical battens. The struts are secured to the base battens of both boxes with M10 6in (150mm) coach bolts.

When assembling, it is best to cut the wall battens to length first, drill their bolt holes (at the height you require—the boxes should be spaced about 12in/300mm apart), then attach to the wall. Lift up the top box, rest it on the sill and secure it with the bolts. Attach the diagonal struts, then slot in and secure the lower box. Finish the unit with paint or apply a preservative stain.

ROCKERY

A rock garden can create a focal point in a flat, otherwise dull plot. But it shouldn't just resemble an untidy heap of stones—plan it carefully to suit its surroundings so it becomes an authentic rocky outcrop for alpine plants and shrubs.

SITING THE ROCKERY

The rockery must be constructed on prepared foundations, so that it looks balanced, won't slump and will drain adequately—important to the health and welfare of the plants. Choose the best site for the rockery: although it is suited to most environments, aim for an area that lies at a slight gradient, but not so steep that the rocks slip and the earth is washed away by rain.

Rockery plants generally favour a sunny situation, so avoid areas beneath deciduous trees, which shed their leaves in winter.

BUYING MATERIALS

The rockery should be made up from various sized natural stones, which you can obtain from stone merchants and some garden centres. In general, choose local stone, so that the rock garden will blend in more easily with other features. If this isn't available, soft, porous limestone or sandstone is a good alternative, because it improves drainage from the site and weathers to interesting shapes.

For a modest-sized rockery about 10ft (3m) across, rising 24in (600mm) above ground level, you will probably need at least 25cwt (1,500kg) of stone. Order a mixture of different sizes and shapes and if you can get them, pick large, flattish slabs as opposed to rounded boulders, which are more difficult to set in place.

Don't use ordinary soil when making a rockery; instead, prepare a mixture of topsoil (or loam-based compost) and ¼in

Top: *Construct the first tier of the rockery, starting with the largest 'keystone'. Set smaller stones to form the arms of an L-shape spanning from this, leaning the stones into the gradient. Add a free-draining soil/grit mixture to the outcrop.*
Centre: *Add further rocky outcrops, following the same L-shape format of the first, and add more soil/grit mixture.*
Above: *The final tier of the rockery comprises a pinnacle of small stones. Plant out as required with alpines and shrubs.*

(6mm) grit, which you can obtain from larger garden centres. This assures good drainage for the plants, discourages weed growth and helps to bind the rocks in place.

Mark out the position of the rockery on the ground by scribing with a spade, then, when you are satisfied with its shape and size, excavate about 6in (150mm) of topsoil. Set this aside to re-use for the grit mix.

Compact the base of the excavation by tramping with the heels of your boots, then mix up some grit and soil or compost in the ratio 5 parts soil : 1 part grit. Proportion the ingredients using a spade and mix on a patch of clear ground near the hole. Add the mixture to the hole to within about 2in (50mm) of ground level.

POSITIONING THE ROCKS

The most successful design for a rockery is composed of a series of L-shaped rocky outcrops, decreasing in size from a broad base to a pinnacle at the back. Each terrace contains a large

Above: *A rock garden filled with miniature shrubs and alpines suggests a natural outcrop blending well with many styles of garden.*

keystone at the elbow of the outcrop, which prevents the other stones—which become smaller as they stem from it—from slipping down the gradient.

Roll the largest keystone into place at the base of the foundation and angle it back into the bank slightly. Pack soil underneath it, then add smaller stones to make the arms, again tilted back towards the centre of the rockery. Cover about one quarter of the stones for a firm support.

Fill the lower outcrop with soil and grit mix, rake it level, then tread it flat. Build the second and subsequent outcrops on top in the same way, setting each about 12in (300mm) behind the preceding one. Form a pinnacle from a cluster of medium-sized stones, then cover the exposed soil/gravel with a 1in (25mm) thick layer of grit alone.

Leave the rockery for a fortnight before planting out, to allow the ground to settle slightly.

GARDEN POND

If you find appealing the idea of a placid pool of water gracing your garden, consider creating a pond and stocking it with fish and water-plants. Choose a prefabricated version for rapid results, or sculpt one to your own design using flexible liners.

TYPES OF POND

Forget the idea of moulding a pond in concrete—it is a material prone to cracking and leaking and suffers especially at the hands of frost. Pre-formed ponds, however, are quick and easy to install and, despite limiting you to the sizes and shapes in which they are made, it is possible to disguise their origins. For a stepped pond, plump for a rigid glass fibre shell; although costly, they are tough, long-lasting and available in a range of contours with various depths, ranging from 8 x 6ft (2·4 x 1·8m) to a substantial 16 x 11ft (4·8 x 3·6m). In their disfavour, it's necessary to dig the hole to precisely the same profile. Semi-rigid linings, moulded in plastic, are cheaper—and it is not necessary to mimic the profile.

Flexible liners, made of butyl rubber, offer durability and the ability to exercise creativity. The sides of the pond need to be set at an angle of about 60° to prevent them caving in, which increases the size of a deep pond. Work out the size of liner by adding twice the pond depth to its length and width.

Site the feature away from trees as leaves will clog it and their roots may damage it.

DIGGING THE HOLE

Mark out the overall shape of the pond on the ground using string. Remove the topsoil or turfs. With a flexible liner, dig the site to shape and depth, incorporating broad shelves. With a rigid or semi-rigid shell, measure the depth of the first shelf on the

Above: *Dig out the earth to the rough shape of the pond, forming definite shelves, then line the base with 1¼in (30mm) of sand.*

mould, add about 1½in (35mm) for bedding sand and dig to this level from the edge. Use a spirit level and batten to check that the shelf is at the correct depth. At the first shelf, measure its width, mark in the hole then dig to the next level.

Remove all sharp stones and flatten any bumps, then spread a 1½in (35mm) thick layer of sand over the surface. To fit a rigid liner, place it in the hole and check its level. Shake to settle it; add more sand under the rim.

To fit a sheet liner, unfold the material over the hole. Place bricks at intervals around the rim then add water from a hose; as the weight of the liquid pushes the liner into the profile, pleat the edges, then cut off the surplus.

Finish the edges of the pond by bedding paving slabs on a mortar mix of 1 part cement: 4 parts sand. Allow the slabs to overhang the edge by 2in (50mm).

Right: *A pump submerged in the pond can supply water to the waterfall, and then back to the pond for a natural effect.*

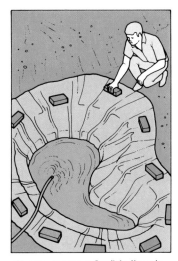

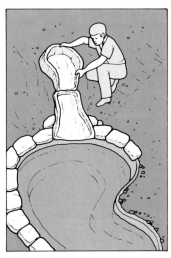

Above: *Drape a flexible liner in the hole, held with weights at the edges. Fill the pond from a hose, easing the liner in gently.*

Above: *Semi-rigid polyethylene waterfall mouldings can be set at the side of the pond to discharge into it, and are bedded in sand.*

BARBECUES

Dining outdoors has its own special pleasures, but you don't have to make do with a humble campside arrangement when it comes to preparing culinary treats—build a barbecue that's every bit as efficient and convenient for the chef as the kitchen cooker. There are numerous styles of barbecue you can make, whether you want a simple temporary surface for grilling a few snacks for the family or a permanent, sturdy unit incorporating seating and serving facilities for summertime entertaining.

BARBECUE BASICS

Whatever style of barbecue you decide to construct, bear in mind some basic requirements for safe, efficient cooking. The grill area should be at a convenient height that allows you to cook comfortably from either a standing or seated position. Avoid a very low barbecue or you will have to crouch down to attend to the food—and you and your fellow diners will be enveloped in smoke.

Siting the barbecue is important for your comfort, your neighbours' good will and for safety from the

risk of fire. First, don't confine the barbecue to a remote area unless you are prepared to traipse to and from the house clutching utensils, crockery and food.

Secondly, consider the likely annoyance to your neighbours and position the barbecue where it is not likely to waft smoke through their open living-room window. Thirdly, beware of placing the unit directly below overhanging trees or bushes, which could catch light—and would certainly suffer from the intense heat. Likewise, do not site the grill near open windows, where curtains could catch fire on the hot coals.

So far as the efficiency of the barbecue is concerned, the charcoal needs a free supply of fresh air to burn properly, so an updraught is usual.

LOOSE-BRICK BARBECUE

If you don't relish learning the skills of bricklaying just to build a barbecue that will only be used when the weather's fine,

Below: *Build a permanent barbecue unit in your garden if you're keen on cooking out; provision for a food preparation area makes it self-contained from the kitchen.*

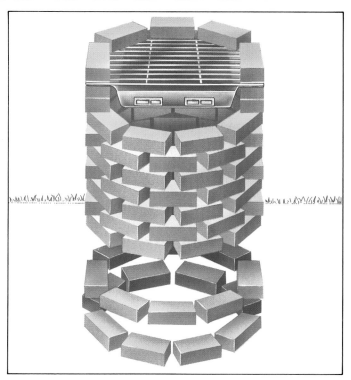

Above: *For a temporary barbecue, construct a loose-bond brick unit. This one is kitted out with proprietary grill and accessories designed for a DIY assembly.*

take the easy way out and construct the unit without mortar. A loose-brick barbecue is an efficient structure—the honeycomb walls allow plenty of air flow to the cooking area—and it is easy to make in just a few hours, and even easier to dismantle.

You can design a round, octagonal—even triangular—unit with matching table and chairs (topped with plywood boards), if you prefer. To make a full-size unit you will need about 100 bricks in your choice of finish. There is no real need to choose expensive types, but if the unit is going to be left outside all year round, however, it is best to pick a type that can withstand some weathering.

STACKING THE BRICKS

To build the barbecue, simply arrange the first course of bricks on a hard, flat surface in your chosen shape, with small 2in (50mm) gaps between each. Lay the second course on top, staggering the joints, then stack subsequent courses on top in this way until you reach grill level. Avoid building too slim a unit, or the bricks will become unstable with height. Don't make the unit too broad, or the walls will collapse inwards.

Fit a sheet of mild steel (bought from a builders' merchants and cut to the size you want) over the bricks for burning the fuel, then continue building another few courses before fitting a grille on which to cook—a slatted tray reclaimed from an old cooker is ideal for this. Another three or four courses forming a windshield completes the barbecue.

BUILD A BARBECUE UNIT

This practical brick-built design
is basically a U-shaped unit
with a grill, charcoal tray and
utensil shelf set within. Special
features include three adjustable
cooking heights, a built-in
windshield and an integral timber
table. Built on a concrete strip
foundation (see page 14), the
walls are only half a brick thick,
and use a standard running
or stretcher bond: the bricks are
laid end to end with alternate
courses staggered so that no
vertical joints align. The end
bricks of alternate courses are
cut in half to maintain the bond,
while to turn the corner into the
back wall, whole bricks are
laid at right-angles to the side
wall and the bond continued.

The table base brickwork is
toothed into holes in one side
of the main structure. The holes
are formed in every fourth course
by using half bricks instead of
whole bricks where the side
wall meets the end wall.

The whole unit should be
designed to fit round any grill that
is available—perhaps salvaged
from an old cooker—and the
dimensions adjusted accordingly.
It is worth laying four or five brick
courses dry to check that the
bonding will work out correctly.

LAYING THE BRICKWORK

To lay the bricks, trowel a screed
of mortar centrally on the concrete
foundation strip. Set up strings
and pegs (see page 19) as a
guide to laying the courses
straight, then position the end
bricks first.

Check that the bricks are level
by spanning their tops with a
long spirit level, then fill in with
more bricks. Trowel mortar on top
and lay the second course. Continue in this way for subsequent
courses.

Use a gauge rod marked off in
brick-plus-joint increments (see
page 21) to make sure the

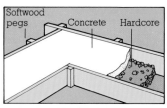

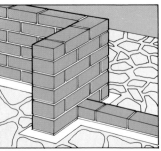

Top: *The foundations are laid in
a 4in (100mm) trench lined with a
timber formwork. Lay 2in (50mm)
of hardcore and fill with concrete.*
Above: *The use of half bricks
in the side wall allows the table
base to be keyed in.*

courses are rising evenly,with
consistent mortar joints. Hold the
spirit level or a long straight-
edged batten diagonally across
the brick faces to check that the
walls are not bowing outwards.

When you reach the tenth
course, embed four 6in (150mm)
long pieces of ¼in (6mm) diameter
mild steel rod in the mortar joint,
so they protrude beyond the
side and back walls to support

Below: *Steel brackets plugged into
the brickwork secure the table.*

Above: *The completed barbecue. It features a built-in windshield, adjustable cooking heights, utensil shelf and serving table.*

the charcoal tray. When you lay the next course, the rods will be sandwiched between the bricks. Repeat this procedure at the next three courses to give the three cooking heights: you can then simply slide out the grill and reposition it where required.

Below: *If you prefer, design your own permanent barbecue unit, like this attractive block-built example.*

Set two courses of bricks along the back wall and turn them round onto the sides to make the windshield.

FITTING OUT

Measure up for a panel of thick steel sheet for the charcoal tray, and have it cut to size by the supplier—the larger builders' merchants are the best source for this. Allow 2in (50mm) extra from front to back, and bend this at right-angles to form a rim to contain the charcoal. Clamp the sheet between two timber battens, held in a vice, and hammer the flap around this former using a mallet.

Make up the table top from three pieces of 6 x 1in (150 x 25mm) softwood, spaced 1in (25mm) apart and fixed together with short lengths attached across their ends using corrugated metal fasteners, which you simply hammer across the joint. Screw the top to metal angle brackets plugged and screwed to the masonry base.

The utensil shelf is a panel of ¾in (19mm) thick chipboard resting on softwood battens screwed to the sides and back of the barbecue unit.

GARDEN TABLE

If you decamp to the garden during the warm summer months you will need to furnish the patio with a practical arrangement for dining. What is important with outdoor furniture is portability and a means of stowing it away when the weather deteriorates. This octagonal table combines a rigid construction with collapsibility.

MAKING THE TOP

The top is made from a planed softwood perimeter frame with softwood slats; it rests on a stout cross frame into which sturdy dowel legs are fitted, and is braced at the base by a cross-rail. The entire top lifts off, the legs and top frame fold flat and the table can be stacked on edge in the shed or garage when not in use.

An overall diameter of 36in (900mm) is adequate to seat four diners in comfort. The design can be scaled up if required.

MAKING A TEMPLATE

To work out the length of the frame pieces, it is best to make a template: draw a circle on a large sheet of brown paper (or a few sheets taped together), using an improvized pair of compasses made from string with a pin and a pencil tied to opposite ends.

Divide the circle into eight segments. Connect the segmenting lines at the perimeter to draw the octagon. Buy long lengths of 6 x 1in (150 x 25mm) planed softwood and lay over the template to mark the shape of the pieces. Use a sliding bevel to scribe the mitred ends, then cut them to length with a tenon saw. Place the softwood

Below: *The table is made from softwood with stout dowel legs; the top outer frame has a ledge onto which the slats are fixed and the entire assembly locates onto a hinged cross-frame with dowel pins.*

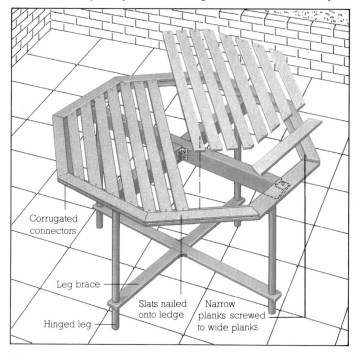

Corrugated connectors

Leg brace

Slats nailed onto ledge

Narrow planks screwed to wide planks

Hinged leg

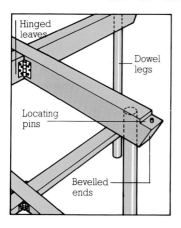

Hinged leaves

Dowel legs

Locating pins

Bevelled ends

Above: *Hinged leaves fold opposite ways; ends are bevelled and notched, with locating pins for securing the top.*

pieces on the template, resting on a flat surface, and butt their ends together. Apply PVA glue to the meeting ends, then secure each joint by hammering corrugated timber connectors into the timber across the joint. Fix two connectors per joint, driving them in dovetail fashion. Now make a second octagon using narrower 4 x 1in (100 x 25mm) timber. Fix these on top of the first frame, outer edges flush, by glueing and screwing from underneath with 1½in (35mm) No. 8 brass screws.

Now, on your template, divide the central area into an equal number of 2in (50mm) wide strips with gaps between. Cut lengths of 2 x ½in (50 x 12mm) planed timber to fit within the narrower frame, nailing them to the ledge formed by a wider outer frame. Sink the nail heads and fill the indents.

MAKING THE CROSS BRACE

Make a cross-brace for the top from 3 x 4in (75 x 100mm) timber: you'll need one length to span the table top, less 3in (75mm) at each end, and two lengths to fit at each side of it. Cut a 3in

(75mm) wide, 1in (25mm) deep notch in each end, onto which the top can slot. Bevel the ends inwards.

Assemble the cross-piece by hingeing the two shorter lengths to the long one: one half folds one way; the other the opposite.

Stick 1in (25mm) long pieces of ½in (12mm) diameter dowel in the centre of the notches and mark matching locating holes on the underside of the table top outer frame—use the template for positioning these.

Drill a 1¼in (30mm) diameter 1¾in (43mm) deep hole in the underside of the cross-piece components—6in (150mm) in from the ends—to take the dowel legs.

LEG ASSEMBLY

To make the legs, cut four 24in (600mm) long pieces of 1¼in (30mm) diameter softwood dowelling. Make the cross-brace from a length of 2½ x 1in (60 x 25mm) planed softwood 5in (125mm) shorter than the top cross-piece. Drill dowel holes 2in (50mm) in from each end.

Slot the legs into the brace so they protrude 3in (75mm) and secure by glueing a 1¼in (30mm) long piece of ⅜in (9·5mm) diameter dowelling through a pre-drilled hole. Give the table a thorough sanding then apply a preservative stain in the colour of your choice followed by several coats of polyurethane varnish.

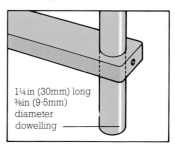

1¼in (30mm) long ⅜in (9·5mm) diameter dowelling

Above: *The 1¼in (30mm) diameter dowel legs slot into holes drilled in each end of the brace.*

GARDEN SEAT

No matter how busy you are, there is always time to take a rest and admire your hard work in the garden from the vantage of a comfy seat.

BUILDING THE PLINTH

The framework rests on a brick plinth. Build the plinth on strip foundations—make a single skin, stretcher-bonded wall four courses high. The inside dimensions take the seat legs.

MAKING THE FRAME

Mark out and cut two side panels from a sheet of sturdy ¾in (19mm) thick exterior grade plywood. Keep the back and base at right-angles to each other, but with pleasing curves, as in the drawings. The front-to-back dimension of the side panels should be equal to the depth of the plinth. The height of the panels should be about 24in (600mm).

You should be able to cut both panels from one 4ft sq (1·2m sq) sheet. Cut one first then use it as a template for cutting the second one accurately.

Use a power jig-saw to cut the ply. This has a thin blade that cuts curves with ease: guide the blade along the waste side of the guideline.

The two panels are connected by three 60in (1·5m) lengths of 4 x 1in (100 x 25mm) planed softwood, which slot into rectangular holes cut in the plywood, and are retained by wedges driven into notches cut in the ends of the rails.

Mark out the positions of the holes on the ply panels: the back rails should be vertically in line, positioned so they'll run along the inner face of the brick plinth's back leaf—that's roughly 4½in (112mm) in from the back edge of the panels. The front rail should be the same distance in from the front edge of the panels. Use a pencil, try square and rule to mark the slots on one sheet of ply, drill a starter hole in each corner for the jigsaw blade, then cut out the waste and try the rails for fit: they should be tight.

Cut four 30in (750mm) long legs from 2in sq (50mm sq) sawn softwood. Lie the front and back lower rails on a flat surface, ends aligned, then place the legs on the rails, at right-angles to

Below: *The garden seat frame is made from heavy duty plywood, cut to form the side panels, with three softwood braces between them, glued and wedged into slots cut in the sides. The legs fit onto the lower rails and slot into the brick plinth.*

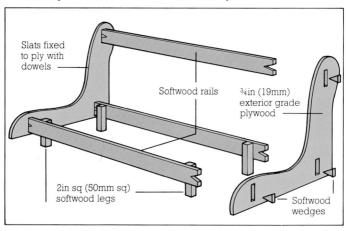

Slats fixed to ply with dowels

Softwood rails

¾in (19mm) exterior grade plywood

2in sq (50mm sq) softwood legs

Softwood wedges

Above: *The seat, complete with brick plinth, is designed to fit into an existing run of walling, perhaps defining a raised planting bed or patio wall. Its slatted surface resembles the familiar park bench.*

them and their ends flush with one edge. Position the legs on the rails so they'll fit tightly into the inner angle of the plinth walls. Strike off the positions of the legs on the rails. Drill five ¼in (6mm) diameter clearance holes in the rails, then drill ⅛in (3mm) pilot holes at corresponding positions on the legs. Apply PVA glue to the meeting faces and screw the rails to the legs.

Now cut four triangular wedges from 1in (25mm) thick planed timber—they should be about 3in (75mm) long by the same deep, tapering to points. Mark out and cut triangular notches, about 1in (25mm) smaller than the

wedges, in each end of the rails.

Slot the rails into the ply panels so their ends are flush with the outer face of the panels, apply PVA adhesive to the notches and wedges, then insert the wedges and tap firmly into the notches to splay the rails slightly, gripping them in the holes. When the glue has set, plane the protruding ends of the wedges flush with the ply.

FIXING THE SLATS

Mark out and cut enough 60in (1·5m) long slats from 2 x ½in (50 x 12mm) planed softwood to clad the seat frame (you'll need about 20), chamfer their top edges with glasspaper, then attach to the ply panels by dowels glued into predrilled holes (made with the aid of a proprietary dowelling jig).

Apply a preservative stain, then slot the legs into the brick plinth.

COMPOST CONTAINER

Compost is ideal for improving your garden's soil—but the heap from which it comes isn't the most attractive item you are likely to encounter. Proprietary bins are sold to contain and conceal the compost, but they can look utilitarian—it is quite straight-forward to make your own, designed especially to blend in well with its surroundings.

MAKING THE PANELS

The timber container is made from slatted panels of sawn softwood, which slot into channels attached to stout posts fixed in the ground, marking the area of the fixture. All timber should be thoroughly treated with preservative before use, or bought pressure-impregnated.

The panels can be raised in the channels or removed completely for access to the compost. There are two sections in the container: one for compost in use; the other for compost that is maturing. The gaps formed by the offset planking assure necessary flow

of air to the centre of the heap.

To make a panel, cut two lengths of 1in sq (25mm sq) soft-wood to the height you want the container: 4ft (1·2m) is adequate. Mark out and cut eight 5ft (1·5m) lengths of 6 x 1in (150 x 25mm) softwood for the cladding. Starting at one end, nail four strips of cladding to the battens, their ends flush with the outer edge, spaced 6in (150mm) apart. Turn the assembly over and nail the other four panels to the batten, but offset them so that they fill the gaps left by the cladding on the opposite side.

Make up seven matching panels to complete the container.

SETTING THE POSTS

The posts which form the corners of the container are 6ft (1·8m) lengths of 4in sq (100mm sq) sawn softwood. The extra length allows for 2ft (600mm) to be sunk in the ground—you can set them in concrete or anchor them in metal fence spikes.

Cut enough 4ft (1·2m) lengths

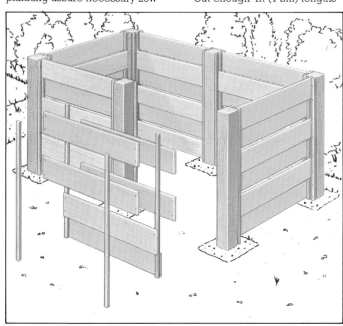

of 1in sq (25mm sq) softwood to make channelling for the posts: you will need four per post, except for the central back and front posts, which require three pairs. Simply set the strips along the length of the posts, flush with the edges and aligned with the tops, leaving 2in (50mm) gaps between.

Fix the strips to the posts using

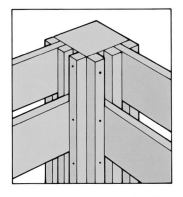

Left: *The compost container is built on a modular basis, whereby stout posts are sunk in the ground in concrete and fitted with channelling, into which the timber walls are slotted.*
Above: *The slatted panels are made from planks nailed on each side of slim battens; they slot within the post channels.*

Above: *Adapt the basic design of the compost container to suit your needs and the space you have available. Twin containers mean one load of compost can be maturing while that in the neihbouring section is in use.*

2in (50mm) long galvanized nails at 4in (100m) intervals. Make sure the channelling is parallel or the panels won't slide freely.

If the container is to be fixed directly against a wall or fence, you can omit the channelling on the sides of the three back posts and nail the battens of the two back panels directly to the posts.

To assemble the container, mark out the site with strings and pegs and indicate where each post is to stand—they'll be fractionally over 5ft (1·5m) apart, the extra allowance being included for fitting tolerance.

Dig the post holes, place hardcore in the base and set the posts in place. Pour in concrete to retain them, after checking that they are perfectly vertical in both planes by holding your spirit level against adjacent sides. Alternatively, simply drive in fence spikes and insert the posts.

Slot the panels into the channels and your compost container is ready to receive its first load.

SANDPIT AND POOL

Children need a special zone in the garden—otherwise your prize plot will soon resemble a lunar landscape. Bring the beach to your garden with this dual sandpit and paddling pool, cleverly designed so that water and sand never meet.

THE BASIC FRAME

The 'bow-tie' shape of the pool-cum-pit is formed using only four pieces of 6 x 1in (150 x 25mm) planed softwood—commonly used for floorboards. The main frame pieces are connected with a simple cross-halving joint and the triangular segments completed with butt-jointed side pieces.

You will need one 10ft (3m) long piece of timber for the main spine, a 5ft (1·5m) piece for the cross-piece and one 11ft (3·3m) piece, which you cut in half later, for the sides. Measure the

half-way marks on the cross-pieces. Lay them on the floor, side-by-side, and align the centre marks. Measure and mark parallel lines against a try square ½in (12mm) from each side of the centre line; this gives the width of the joint. Set a marking gauge to half the timber thickness—nominally 3in (75mm), but measure the actual wood—and scribe between the parallel lines drawn across the pieces, with the stock of the tool held tight against the edge of the timber. This indicates the depth of the joint.

To cut the joint, saw down the width lines to the depth line

Below: *The pool/sandpit unit is made from two lengths of timber joined with a cross-halving joint, fitted onto two end panels, mitred as shown. Cover both sandpit and pool (made from a butyl pond liner) with a triangle of thin wood lipping for a neat appearance.*

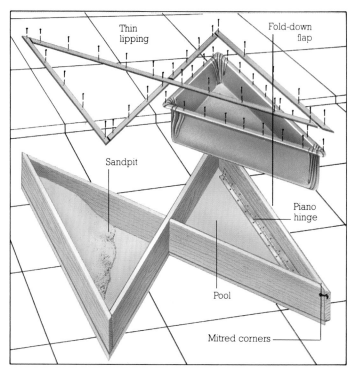

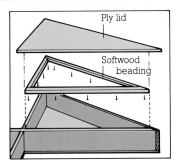

Ply lid

Softwood beading

Above: *The two lids are each made from plywood triangles, each with a wooden rim nailed onto it, so it can be slotted onto the unit's walls.*

using a tenon saw, then use a coping saw to cut along the scribed line, so removing the waste. Square up the corners with a chisel, then slot the two notches together.

So that the side pieces will fit against the cross-assembly, mitre their ends: use a sliding bevel to set the angles. Transfer one mitre to the top end of the uncut timber, at the centre. This way you can cut two matching mitres at the same time as cutting the pieces to length. Continue the line down both faces of the pieces, then saw the wood in half. If you have a circular saw with an adjustable sole plate this job is much easier: simply set the saw blade to the angle required. Cut the mitres on the other ends of both pieces.

Dovetail-nail through the cross pieces into the sides to hold the frame together. Optionally, you

Below: *This cross-sectional view shows how to sink the unit into an area of paving slabs to cope with any spillages of sand and water.*

can hinge the side piece on the pool section, so that the water can be emptied out: fit a plastic piano hinge (cut to length with a hacksaw) along the lower edge and retain with hook fasteners.

The frame is completed—and stiffened—with two triangles of ½in (12mm) thick exterior-quality chipboard screwed to the underside of the softwood assembly. Drill ³⁄₁₆in (4mm) clearance holes through the chipboard at 6in (150mm) intervals, then attach it to the frame with 1in (25mm) No.8 brass countersunk screws. Trim the inner corner of the triangles where they meet at the halving joint.

MAKING THE LIDS

It is preferable to fit lids to the pool and pit both for safety and to prevent cats or dogs fouling the sand. Cut two triangles of ½in (12mm) thick exterior quality plywood to fit over the frame, chopping off the inner corners as with the base panels. Screw a rim of ¾in sq (19mm sq) beading to the underside of the lids, set back from their edges by 1in (25mm) and butt-joined. The lids slot onto the tops of the pit and pool.

Finally, line the base of the pool with a sheet of thick butyl rubber pond liner or heavy-gauge polythene. Fold the sheet neatly at the corners and tack an overlap to the top edge of the main frame. Leave the corner fold loose at the fold-down flap. To complete the unit and to neaten the top edge of the frame, pin thin lipping over the top (adding a separate piece for the fold-down flap).

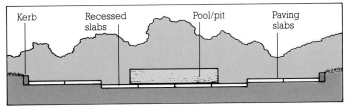

Kerb   Recessed   Pool/pit   Paving
            slabs   slabs

CLIMBING FRAME

Kids love to climb and have the uncanny knack of falling off scaled heights. This climbing frame provides a safe, secure structure for them to air their adventurous urges—and it is easy to build with readily available tough metal fittings and steel tubing.

USING CLAMPS

Proprietary galvanized cast iron fittings and couplings can be used along with steel tubing to create a versatile adaptable framework that is tough, durable and safe in use.

The fittings—Kee Klamps are one commonly available system —comprise tee-sockets, single sockets, elbows, straight couplers and end cups, which you can use to style the frame as you wish. The photographs show just one combination of fittings which you can adapt in numerous ways.

Tubes and fittings—available direct from the manufacturer, from DIY stores, builder's merchants or scaffolding suppliers—are made in six diameters from ⅞in (21mm), up to 2⅜in (60mm), although the larger ones are best for your climbing frame. The fittings are slotted onto the smooth-walled steel tube and the clamps tightened using an Allen key. The tubing can be cut to length using a hacksaw.

If you don't like the dull grey finish of tubing and fittings, you can colour them with a tough aerosol spray paint.

ERECTING FRAMES

So that the climbing frame is anchored safely to the ground, with no risk of toppling over, it is essential to set the main uprights in holes in the ground. Set the tubing in sockets of larger

Below: *Construct the climbing frame on site, slotting the lengths of tubing into the clamps; retain them with Allen screws. Work out your basic design first to save time.*

diameter tubing—the fit need not be precise—which are themselves encased in concrete: you will then be able to dismantle the structure easily, pull out the posts and store the entire frame.

Sketch out a diagram of how you want the finished frame to appear, then transfer the plan to the ground, marking the overall shape with strings and using pegs to indicate the uprights.

Dig 12in (300mm) deep holes about 12in (300mm) square, line them with hardcore, then position 12in (300mm) lengths of steeel tubing in place with bricks, then pour concrete into the hole around them. To ensure that the sockets are set perfectly vertical, slot in a length of tubing and hold a spirit level against it at intervals around its circum-

Below: *The climbing frame can assume many shapes and sizes, depending on your imagination. Avoid overhanging sections, though, and ensure a broad base for stability in use.*

ference; tap the post to align it, and prop it up with temporary wooden struts. Leave the concrete to harden fully for about seven days before construction begins.

It is best to construct the frame on site, with the main posts in position, then add the cross-pieces. Just slot on the required fitting, slide it to the position you want the rail to be, but don't tighten its clamp. Fit a second clamp opposite the first, measure between them and cut a length of tubing to fit. Slot the tubing into the sockets—you might have to remove the sockets from the posts, as there may not be sufficient tolerance for slotting in the tubing—and tighten the clamps fully with the Allen key of the correct size (which depends on the size of fitting you choose).

Accidents are bound to happen, so minimize injury by covering the base of the frame with a 3in (75mm) layer of sand, contained within the play area by timber formwork fixed to stakes.

INDEX

PICTURE CREDITS

Artists
Copyright of the illustrations on the pages following the artists' names is the
property of Salamander Books Ltd.
Kuo Kang Chen: 25, 26, 27, 28, 29, 30, 31, 34, 36, 37, 41, 45, 46, 49, 51, 52, 53,
54, 55, 58, 60, 61, 63, 72, 73
Steve Cross: 10, 11, 12, 13, 14, 15, 16, 17, 19, 20-21, 23, 56-57, 66, 67,
68, 69, 70, 71
Clifford and Wendy Meadway: 64-65

Photographs
The publishers wish to thank the following photographers who have supplied
photographs for the book. The photographs have been credited by page
number and position on the page: B (Bottom), T (Top), BL (Bottom Left) etc.
Cement & Concrete Association: 15 (B), 17 (C)
Eric Crichton: Endpapers, Title Page, 6, 18, 29 (C), 31 (CR), 38-39 (T), 43 (C),
48, 59, 61, 62, Back cover (B)
Forest Fencing Ltd: 25 (T), 30 (B)
Kee Klamps Ltd: 74, 75
Peter McHoy: 21, 24, 25 (BL), 29 (B), 39 (C), 39 (B), 40, 42 (T), 43 (T), 45 (C), Back
cover (TL, TR)
Harry Smith Collection: 8-9, 32, 33 (C), 44, 47, 50, 64, 71 (T)
David Squire: 33 (B), 41 (T)

PRINTED IN BELGIUM BY

INTERNATIONAL BOOK PRODUCTION